My World
ADVENTURES IN TIME AND PLACE

James A. Banks

Barry K. Beyer

Gloria Contreras

Jean Craven

Gloria Ladson-Billings

Mary A. McFarland

Walter C. Parker

NATIONAL
GEOGRAPHIC
SOCIETY

THIS DOLL WAS MADE IN THE
1920S. MANY THINGS TODAY ARE
DIFFERENT FROM HOW THEY
WERE LONG AGO. BUT CHILDREN
STILL HAVE TOYS THAT ARE
SPECIAL TO THEM.

Macmillan
McGraw-Hill

New York   Farmington

PROGRAM AUTHORS

Dr. James A. Banks
Professor of Education and Director of the Center for Multicultural Education
University of Washington
Seattle, Washington

Dr. Barry K. Beyer
Professor Emeritus, Graduate School of Education
George Mason University
Fairfax, Virginia

Dr. Gloria Contreras
Professor of Education
University of North Texas
Denton, Texas

Jean Craven
District Coordinator of Curriculum Development
Albuquerque Public Schools
Albuquerque, New Mexico

Dr. Gloria Ladson-Billings
Professor of Education
University of Wisconsin
Madison, Wisconsin

Dr. Mary A. McFarland
Instructional Coordinator of Social Studies, K–12, and Director of Staff Development
Parkway School District
Chesterfield, Missouri

Dr. Walter C. Parker
Professor and Program Chair for Social Studies Education
University of Washington
Seattle, Washington

NATIONAL GEOGRAPHIC SOCIETY
Washington, D.C.

PROGRAM CONSULTANTS

Daniel Berman
Asian Studies Specialist
Coordinator of Social Studies
Bedford Central Schools
Bedford, New York

Dr. Khalid Y. Blankinship
Affiliated Scholar, Council on Islamic Education
Fountain Valley, California
Assistant Professor of Religion
Temple University
Philadelphia, Pennsylvania

Dr. John Bodnar
Professor of History
Indiana University
Bloomington, Indiana

Dr. Roberto R. Calderón
Department of Ethnic Studies
University of California at Riverside
Riverside, California

Dr. Sheilah Clarke-Ekong
Asst. Professor, Department of Anthropology and Research Associate, Center for International Studies
University of Missouri, St. Louis
St. Louis, Missouri

Dr. John L. Esposito
Professor of Religion and International Affairs
Georgetown University
Washington, D.C.

Dr. Darlene Clark Hine
John A. Hannah Professor of History
Michigan State University
East Lansing, Michigan

Paulla Dove Jennings
Project Director
The Rhode Island Indian Council, Inc.
Providence, Rhode Island

Dr. Henrietta Mann
Professor of Native American Studies
University of Montana, Missoula
Missoula, Montana

Dr. Gary Manson
Professor, Department of Geography
Michigan State University
East Lansing, Michigan

Dr. Juan Mora-Torrés
Professor of Latin American History
University of Texas at San Antonio
San Antonio, Texas

Dr. Valerie Ooka Pang
Professor, School of Teacher Education
San Diego State University
San Diego, California

Dr. Joseph R. Rosenbloom
Professor, Classics Department
Washington University
St. Louis, Missouri

Dr. Joseph B. Rubin
Director of Reading
Fort Worth Independent School District
Fort Worth, Texas

Dr. Robert M. Seltzer
Professor of Jewish History
Hunter College of The City University of New York
New York, New York

Dr. Peter N. Stearns
Dean, College of Humanities and Social Studies
Carnegie Mellon University
Pittsburgh, Pennsylvania

GRADE-LEVEL CONSULTANTS

Linda Baird Garner
First Grade Teacher
Dudley Elementary School
Fairport, New York

Joan Hinze
First Grade Teacher
Webster Elementary School
Watertown, Wisconsin

Marlene F. Kuskin
Elementary School Teacher
St. Joseph Collinwood Elementary School
Cleveland, Ohio

Gayle B. Morrison
First Grade Teacher
Woodrow Wilson Elementary School
Birmingham, Alabama

Kate Robertson
Assistant Principal
Sneed Elementary School
Houston, Texas

Pamela Shannon
Elementary School Teacher
Graystone School
San Jose, California

CONTRIBUTING WRITERS

Catherine M. Tamblyn
Little Silver, New Jersey

Linda Scher
Raleigh, North Carolina

Acknowledgments

The publisher gratefully acknowledges permission to reprint the following copyrighted material:

Excerpts from **It's My Earth Too** by Kathleen Krull. Copyright 1992. Used by permission of Dell Books, a division of Bantam Doubleday Dell Publishing Group, Inc.

Excerpt from **Houses and Homes** by Ann Morris. Copyright 1992 by Ann Morris. Lothrop, Lee & Shepard, a division of William Morrow & Company.

(continue on page R18)

Macmillan/McGraw-Hill

A Division of The **McGraw·Hill** Companies

CONTENTS

UNIT THREE
72

People at Work

UNIT FOUR
102

Our World

UNIT FIVE
142

It Happened in America

UNIT SIX
182

Americans Celebrate

REFERENCE SECTION

FEATURES

CHARTS & GRAPHS

MAPS

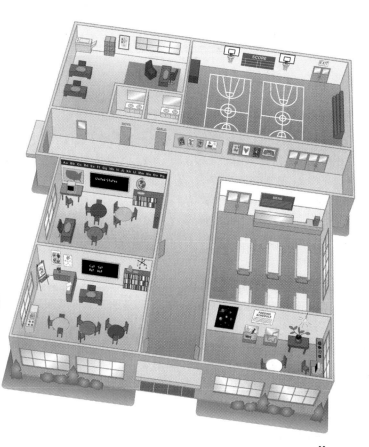

YOUR TEXTBOOK
at a glance

Your book is called *My World: Adventures in Time and Place.* It has many parts.

NATIONAL GEOGRAPHIC

Look at Your World

What does this place have that other places don't have?

What makes the beach a fun place to be?

▲

One special part of your book is called **Look at Your World**. It shows places in our country.

Your book has six units. Each unit has many lessons. You will learn new things in each lesson.

▶

LESSON **1**

Here We Are

This is Tim's first day at school.
His school is in Austin, Texas.
"Welcome," says Mrs. Rose.
Mrs. Rose is Tim's teacher.

4

Some units **Close with a Story.** Others close with a poem or a song.

CITIZENSHIP
Making Choices

A Playground Problem

Our class played outside today. Not everyone got along.

Look at the pictures. Why did we argue? What can we do to get along better tomorrow?

We should put these things away.

Why should we? We didn't use them last.

from
IT'S MY EARTH, TOO
HOW I CAN HELP THE EARTH STAY ALIVE

CITIZENSHIP
Making a Difference

CALIFORNIA
Los Angeles

Tim sat next to Ann. She drew a picture of her house. Her house is red. Tim drew a picture of his house. His house is white.

Ralph Sanders is the teacher who started the club. He takes the cans to a place where they can be reused. The club gets paid a little money for each can. Then they use the money to buy trees for the schoolyard.

So far the Earth Niños club has bought and planted 50 trees. Yvette says, "I feel happy because we are making the earth feel better."

Some special lessons tell about people who are Making a Difference. Others tell about Making Choices.

PICTURE GLOSSARY

Dictionary of GEOGRAPHIC WORDS

HILL Land that is higher than the land around it, but lower than a mountain.

PLAIN Flat land.

LAKE Body of water with land all around it.

Look at the back of your book. The Dictionary of Geographic Words and **Picture Glossary** tell what words mean.

NATIONAL GEOGRAPHIC

Look at Your World

What does this place have that other places don't have?

What makes the beach a fun place to be?

How do you get to school in the morning?

What do people do to help plants grow?

How does this boy know where he is?

UNIT ONE

Where We Live

Key Words

neighborhood

map

community

state

country

Earth

Here We Are

This is Tim's first day at school.
His school is in Austin, Texas.
"Welcome," says Mrs. Rose.
Mrs. Rose is Tim's teacher.

4

Tim sat next to Ann. She drew a picture of her house. Her house is red. Tim drew a picture of his house. His house is white.

"What did you see on your way to school today?" asks Mrs. Rose.

Tim saw a library. Ann saw a church. She also saw a firehouse.

"I live across the street from a firehouse," says Tim.

"You both live in the same **neighborhood**," says Mrs. Rose. "A neighborhood is a place where people live, work, and play. You live near each other. So you are neighbors."

Tim and Ann also saw houses and a park on their way to school. These places are in their neighborhood.

? Study

1. What is a neighborhood?

2. What are some places in your neighborhood?

GEOGRAPHY SKILLS
Using Maps

Here are some rooms in Tim and Ann's school. You can see what the rooms would look like without a roof. Can you find the lunchroom?

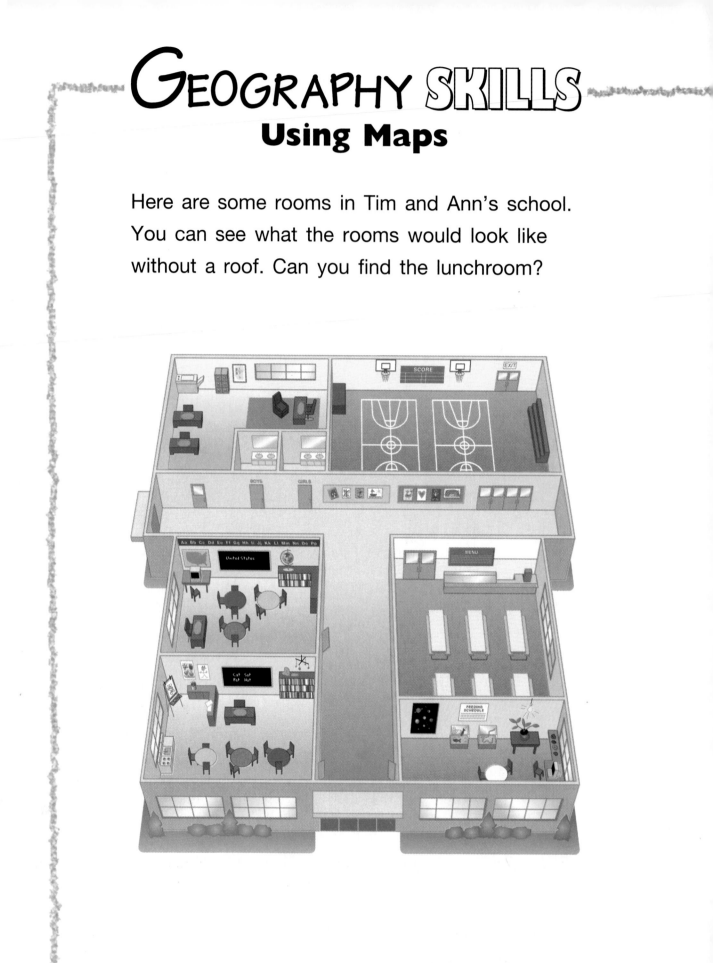

This is a **map** of the school. A map is a drawing of a place. Mrs. Rose's class is next to Mr. Green's class.

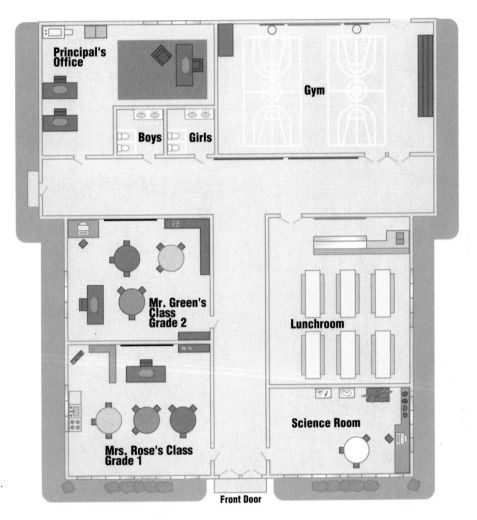

Trying the Skill

Use the map to answer these questions.

1. Is the front door near or far from the gym?
2. Is Mrs. Rose's class to the left or the right of the Science room?
3. How would a map of your classroom be helpful to you?

Our Homes Are in Neighborhoods

Tim and Ann's class is making a poster. It shows homes in neighborhoods. Look at the different kinds of homes.

10

Neighborhoods are different too. Mrs. Rose says, "Some neighborhoods have many homes and stores. Others have only a few places."

This is Ann's house. Tim and his brother David ride by her house.

"Is this where you live?" Tim asks. "I knew your house was red. But I did not know your address."

An address tells the number of a house. It also tells the name of a street.

The number of Ann's house is 56.
The name of the street is Elm Street.

"My address is 56 Elm Street," Ann says.

Tim tells Ann his address. His address is 12 Oak Street. "Now you can find my house!" he says.

1. What are some different kinds of houses?

2. How can addresses help you find places?

CITIZENSHIP
Making a Difference

Rochester

MICHIGAN

Caitlin and Compass

Meet Caitlin Littmann. Caitlin loves dogs and likes helping people. Caitlin and her family joined the Puppy Program at Leader Dogs for the Blind.

The Puppy Program sent a puppy to Caitlin's family in Rochester, Michigan. Caitlin named the puppy Compass. A compass helps people find their way.

Someday Compass will help people who cannot see. She will help them cross busy streets, shop in stores, and visit friends.

It is Caitlin's job to help Compass get used to people. She takes the dog to places in her neighborhood. Compass must learn to be around people without barking or biting.

One day Compass will go to live with a blind person. "I will be sad when Compass leaves our house," says Caitlin. But she will also be very proud of Compass.

Neighborhoods Are in Communities

We all live in neighborhoods. We also live
in bigger places called **communities**.
Many neighborhoods make up a community.

Meg lives far away from Tim and Ann.
She lives near a town called Bend, Oregon.
A town is a small community.

Meg lives on a ranch. A ranch is a big farm. Meg's family raises horses and cattle.

Ranches are far apart from each other. Meg cannot see her neighbor's house from her ranch.

Paul lives far away from Meg. He lives in a city. A city is a big community. Paul lives in the city of Richmond, Virginia.

Many people live and
work in Richmond.
There are many places
to see and things to do.

1. What is a community?

2. Is your community more like
   Meg's or Paul's? Tell why.

Looking from Above

Paul and his father took a trip on a plane. They looked down at a community. This is what they saw.

This is a map of the same community.
What do you see?

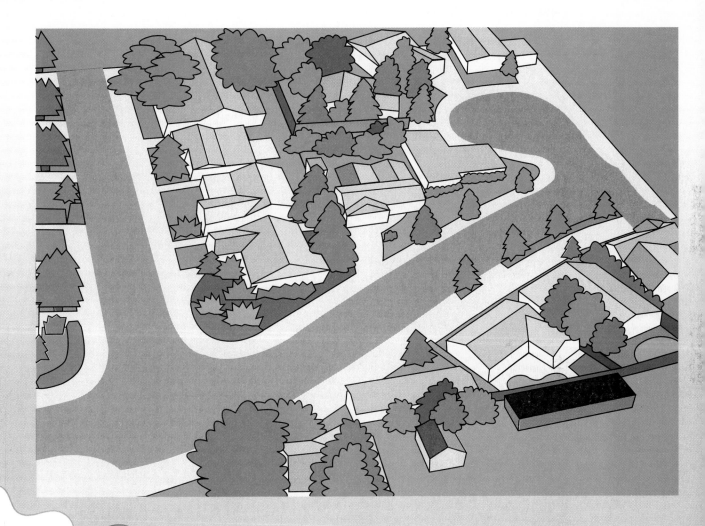

1. How is the map like the picture?
   How is it different?

2. What would you see if you looked at
   your community from a plane?

Using Map Keys

Many maps use symbols. Symbols are small drawings that stand for real things. What things do these symbols stand for?

Maps with symbols have a **map key**. The map key tells what each symbol means.

This is a map of Jim's community. Look at the map key. The swings are a symbol for a playground.

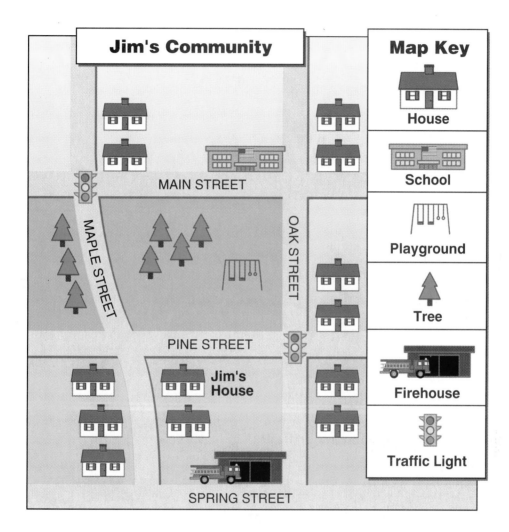

Trying the Skill

Use the map and the map key to answer these questions.

1. Name two buildings on this map.

2. What street is Jim's school on?

3. If you were making a map, what symbols would you use?

We Live in the United States

Communities are in a bigger place called a **state**. This map shows 50 states. They make up our **country**. A country is a land and the people who live there. Our country is the United States of America.

24

NORTH DAKOTA
MINNESOTA
WISCONSIN
MICHIGAN
MICHIGAN
MAINE
VERMONT
NEW HAMPSHIRE
MASSACHUSETTS
NEW YORK
RHODE ISLAND
CONNECTICUT
SOUTH DAKOTA
IOWA
INDIANA
OHIO
PENNSYLVANIA
NEW JERSEY
MARYLAND
DELAWARE
NEBRASKA
ILLINOIS
WEST VIRGINIA
VIRGINIA
VIRGINIA
KANSAS
MISSOURI
KENTUCKY
NORTH CAROLINA
TENNESSEE
SOUTH CAROLINA
OKLAHOMA
ARKANSAS
GEORGIA
MISSISSIPPI
ALABAMA
TEXAS
LOUISIANA
FLORIDA

1. What is the name of our country?

2. What is the difference between a community and a country?

25

Sharing Our Earth

Where do you live? You can answer in many ways.

You live in a home. Your home is part of a neighborhood. Your neighborhood is part of a community. Your community is part of a state. Your state is part of a country.

All countries are part of the world. Another name for the world is **Earth**. Earth is made up of land and water.

A globe is a model of Earth. The blue parts show water. The other colors show land. A globe helps you find places on Earth. Find the land on the globe.

Earth is a very big place. It is shared by all living things. What things in the picture do you know about?

1. What is Earth?

2. Name three different places that you live in.

from

HOUSES
· AND ·
HOMES

by Ann Morris

Photographs by Ken Heyman

The world is full of houses . . .

big houses

little houses

bright houses

white houses

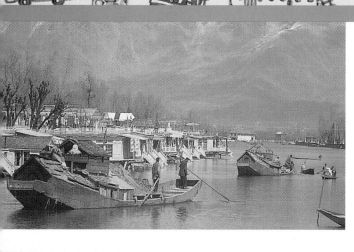

houses that move

and houses that stay

in a row

or all alone

filled with families

just right for one.

UNIT 1 REVIEW

Thinking About Words

Match the words to the pictures.

1. neighborhood   **2.** community   **3.** state
4. country   **5.** Earth

a.
United States

b.

c.
Indiana

d.

e.

Thinking About Ideas

1. What are neighbors?

2. What does an address tell?

3. Name two kinds of communities.

4. Tell how you can live in a state and a country at the same time.

SHARE WITH A FRIEND

Tell about a place that you like in your community. Tell why you like it.

38

Using Skills

Reviewing Using Maps

1. Look at the map below. What does it show?

2. Is the flag near or far from the door?

3. What is to the right of Bob's desk?

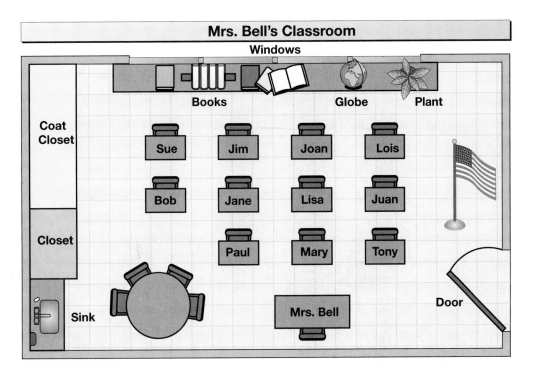

Mrs. Bell's Classroom

Make Your Own!

- Draw a map of the place where you play.
- Add the things you play with.

Using Skills

Reviewing Using Map Keys

1. What does the map show?

2. What symbol stands for the library?

3. How many ranches are shown on the map?

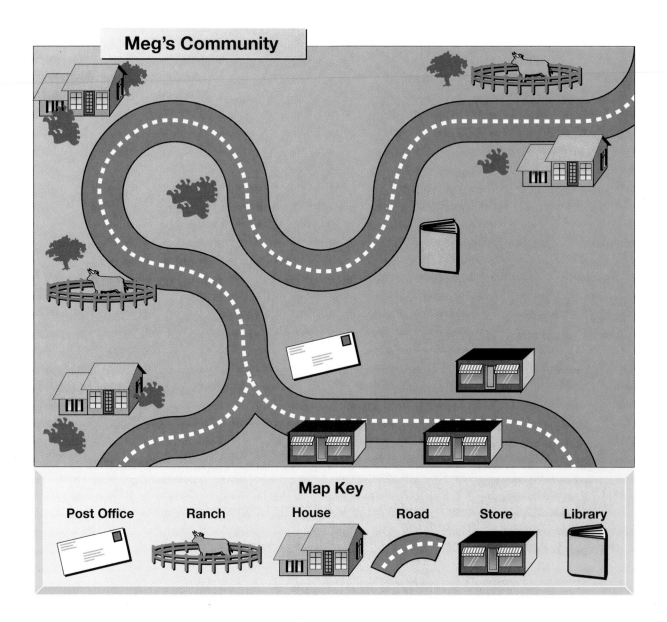

Meg's Community

Map Key

| Post Office | Ranch | House | Road | Store | Library |

Make a "Here I Am" Book

- Draw a picture of yourself. Write your name under the picture.
- Draw a picture of your school. Write the name of your school.
- Draw a picture of some places in your neighborhood.
- Make a cover for your book.
- Staple all the pages together.

Reading on Your Own

You can look for these books at your library.

UNIT TWO

We Belong

Key Words

family

group

rule

law

vote

citizen

President

Family and Friends

My name is Roberto Ramos. Here is my **family**. People in a family care for each other. Families help each other. They play together too.

My grandparents, aunt and uncle, and cousins also belong to my family. Sometimes they visit on special days like birthdays.

Not all families are like mine. Some are bigger. Others are smaller. Sometimes a whole family does not live together.

My family

Roberto

Each family is special. Here are some pictures of my friends and their families.

1. Tell one way that families are the same.

2. Name some people in your family.

People Together

Roberto belongs to many **groups**. People who do things together make up a group. Groups can be big or small.

You and your family are one group. Your class is a group. Your friends are also a group.

People in groups work together. They can play together too. What groups are shown on this page?

study

THINKING SKILLS
Finding Alike and Different

Things that are the same are **alike**. The pictures below are alike. Each shows a group of people. In what other ways are they alike?

Things that are not alike are **different**. How are these pictures different? They are different because they show different sports. In what other ways are they different?

Trying the Skill

Use the pictures on this page to answer the questions.

1. Name two ways the pictures are alike.
2. Name two ways they are different.
3. How can you tell if things are alike or different?

Getting Along

Today is a special day. Police Officer Smith is visiting Roberto's class.

"We all need to get along with others," says Officer Smith. "One way to get along is to follow **rules**. Some rules tell us what to do. Other rules tell us what we should not do."

How We Follow the Rules

"Rules help us get along. They help to keep us safe too," says Officer Smith.

Look at the pictures. Which children are following the rules?

53

"Now let's talk about **laws**," Officer Smith says. "A law is a rule that all people must follow. These pictures show rules and laws. Following them will help keep you safe."

Officer Smith takes the children on a walk.

"Did you know that some laws are on signs?" he asks. "Signs tell you what you should or should not do."

STOP

No cycling

1. How do rules and laws help you get along with others? How do they keep you safe?

2. What new rule do you think your class needs?

CITIZENSHIP
Making Choices

A Playground Problem

Our class played outside today. Not everyone got along.

Look at the pictures. Why did we argue? What can we do to get along better tomorrow?

They won't let anyone use the swings.

No! I was first.

I was first.

57

STUDY SKILLS
Using Charts

Charts show things using words and pictures. The title tells you what the chart is about.

What is a school rule? Read across the chart. "Raise hands" is a school rule. What else is a school rule? Which rules are for home?

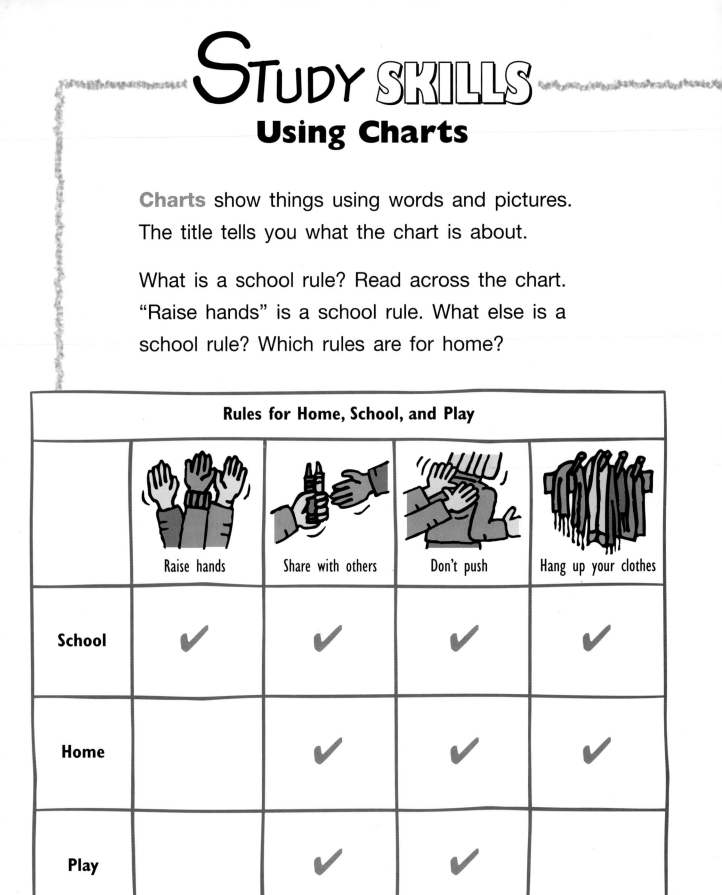

Rules for Home, School, and Play

	Raise hands	Share with others	Don't push	Hang up your clothes
School	✔	✔	✔	✔
Home		✔	✔	✔
Play		✔	✔	

Trying the Skill

This chart shows how Roberto's class will help the teacher. Use it to answer the questions below.

Ways to Help in Class				
	Put away books	Clean chalkboard	Feed class rabbit	Pass paper and crayons
Roberto	✔			
Sara		✔		
Mike				✔
Joan			✔	

1. How many children will help?

2. How will Sara help?

3. Who will feed Peter, the class rabbit?

4. How can charts be helpful?

Your Vote Counts

People may want different things. They can **vote** for what they want. To vote means to choose something.

Roberto's family is voting. What will they do after dinner? Everyone wants to do a puzzle except Roberto's sister.

Roberto's class votes for many things. Today they voted about what to do after lunch.

Their votes are on the chart. What did most children choose?

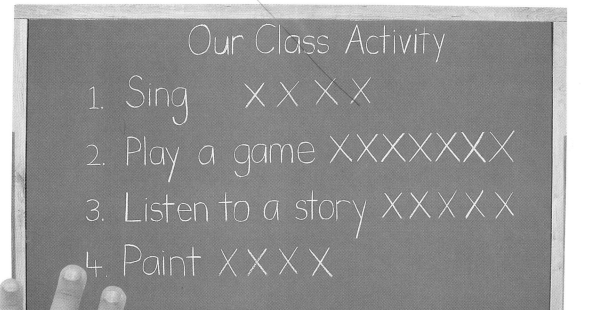

Our Class Activity
1. Sing   X X X X
2. Play a game XXXXXXX
3. Listen to a story X X X X X
4. Paint X X X X

People also vote for leaders. They vote for the person they think will do the best job. Roberto's scout troop voted for Roberto to lead the parade.

Citizens of the United States vote for leaders. A citizen is a member of a country. Everyone born in the United States is a citizen of this country. People who come from other countries can become citizens too.

Grown-up citizens vote for leaders. They vote for the **President** of the United States. The President is the leader of our country.

1. Why do people vote?

2. What kinds of things do you vote about at school and at home?

Family and Friends in Japan

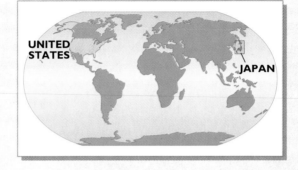

こんにちは

Konnichiwa! That means "hello." My name is Miko Ota. I live in Japan.

This is my family. My grandfather and grandmother live with us. In my family, we follow rules. Rules help us to work together and share.

Here are some of my friends. We wear yellow hats to school. They help keep us safe. Drivers see us when we cross streets.

Children in Japan work very hard in school. I like reading and writing.

After school I go to a special school. I go there to learn more.

Sayonara! Goodbye!

さようなら

1. Miko is part of which groups?

2. How is Miko's life like yours? How is it different?

The World

Words and Music by Ella Jenkins

Oh the world is big ___ and the world is small ___ so there's

lots of room ___ for the short and the tall. Oh the

world is far ___ and the world is wide ___ but there are

is Big, The World is Small

man - y   dif - fer-ent ways to   see   the   oth - er   side. 1.You can
                                                                2.You can

tra - vel   in   a   boat, you can   tra - vel   in   a   plane, you can
tra - vel   on   a   bus,   you can   tra - vel   in   a   train, you can

tra - vel   in   a   dance, you can   tra - vel   in   a   game.
tra - vel   in   a   song,   you can   tra - vel   in   a   name.

UNIT 2 REVIEW

Thinking About Words

Use these words to finish the sentences.

family	**group**	**rules**	**law**
vote	**citizens**	**President**	

1. A _____ is a rule that all people must follow.

2. Members of a _____ love and care for each other.

3. People who do things together are a _____.

4. People get along when they follow _____.

5. To _____ means to choose something.

6. The _____ is the leader of our country.

7. Members of a country are called _____.

Thinking About Ideas

1. What are some things families do together?

2. Why do people belong to groups?

3. How do laws help people?

4. What happens if people don't follow rules?

5. Why is voting a good way to choose something?

What groups are you a part of?
Tell what your groups do together.

Using Skills

Reviewing Using Charts

1. What does the chart show?
2. How does Roberto help at home?
3. Which job do Alma and her dad share?
4. What job does Roberto's mom do?

Ramos Family	Wash and Dry Dishes	Dust	Feed Cat	Set Table	Take Out Garbage
Roberto			✔	✔	
Alma	✔	✔			
Mom					✔
Dad	✔				

JOBS WE DO AT HOME

Make Your Own!

- Make a job chart for a group you belong to. Write a name for your chart.
- Write some of the group's jobs at the top.
- Write the names of the people on the side.
- Mark the boxes to show their jobs.

Using Skills

Reviewing Finding Alike and Different

Use the pictures to answer the questions.

1. In what ways are the pictures alike?

2. In what ways is the girl different in these pictures?

3. In what ways is the family different in these pictures?

4. In what ways are you alike or different from the girl in these pictures?

Gail's Family

Gail's Family

UNIT PROJECT

Making a Puzzle About You

- Think about the groups you belong to.
- Choose one group.
- Draw a picture that shows you with your group.
- Cut your picture into puzzle pieces.
- Have a friend put your puzzle together.

Reading on Your Own

You can look for these books at your library.

People at Work

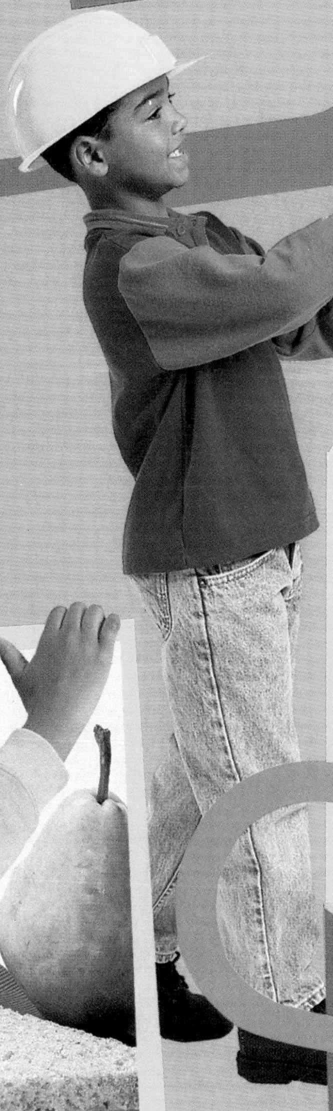

Key Words

job	needs
goods	shelter
service	wants
volunteer	transportation

We Have Jobs

My name is Pam. I have a dog named Rex. It is my **job** to feed him. A job is work that people do.

My mom, dad, and sister Lisa have jobs at home too. We like to share our work.

Mom and Dad also have
jobs away from home.
They are paid money
for their work.

Mom works in a bakery.
Her job is to bake good
things to eat. She is a baker.

My dad works in a hospital. His
job is to take pictures of bones.

Some workers make or grow things.
Things made or grown are called **goods**
My mom makes bread.

Some people do things for other people.
This work is called a **service**. My dad
helps people get well.

Some people work without pay. They are called **volunteers**. Lisa is a volunteer at a hospital.

1. Name a job where people make goods. Name a job that is a service.

2. What jobs do people in your class do?

Our Needs and Wants

All people have **needs**. Needs are things we must have to live. Everyone needs water and food. Apples are my favorite food.

Everyone needs **shelter** too. A shelter is a place to live. Our house is warm when it is cold outside.

People need clothes. Some clothes keep us warm. Some clothes help us to stay cool. Other clothes keep us dry.

People also need love and care. How do people love and care for others?

People have **wants** too. Wants are things we would like to have. We can live without many things that we want. People have different wants. I want dancing lessons. My sister wants a computer. My mom and dad want to take a family trip.

We cannot have all that we want. My family buys the things we need. Then we sometimes get to choose things we want.

Sometimes people cannot buy the things they need. My family helps other people at a special shelter. At the shelter people get food, clothing, and a place to stay.

1. What is the difference between needs and wants?

2. Why do people have to choose what they buy?

CITIZENSHIP
Making Choices

How Should We Spend Our Money?

Pam's class sold cookies at the school fair. They made $50.00. Now the class must choose how to spend the money. How should the class decide? What would your class do with the money?

A tree for our school

New books for
our class

A party!

Give to the
animal shelter

Moving Goods and People

We can buy things we need and want at stores. How do new pants get to a store? Look at these pictures.

Trains are one kind of **transportation**. Transportation moves people or things from one place to another. How do the pants get from the train to the store?

Transportation takes goods to and from
the United States and other countries.
Look at the pictures. What kinds of
transportation do you see?

What kinds of transportation does your community have?

1. What is transportation?

2. How does transportation help people?

THINKING SKILLS
Sorting Things into Groups

Pam wanted to **sort** these pictures into groups. To sort things, she put together things that are alike.

First Pam looked at one picture. Then she looked for others that are like it. She sorted the pictures of the school bus, plane, and boat into one group. She named this group "Transportation."

Look at the other pictures. How are they alike? Tell what group they can make.

Transportation

Trying the Skill

Use the pictures below to answer the questions about sorting.

1. What groups can you make with these pictures?
2. How are the things in each group alike?
3. Name things in your classroom that can be sorted into groups.

About Money

We use coins and paper money to buy
things. Money comes in different amounts.
Can you find a nickel on this page?
How much is a nickel worth?

In the United States paper money is made in Washington, D.C. It is printed on big paper with special ink.

Our country's coins are made in places called mints. Philadelphia has the biggest mint in the world.

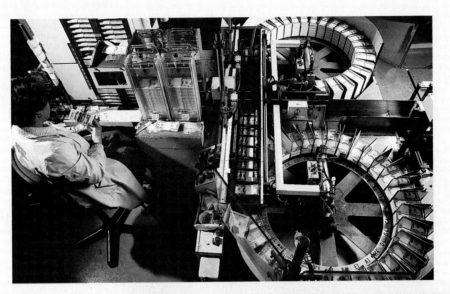

1. Name some amounts money comes in.

2. How do you think we would pay for things if we didn't use coins or paper money?

Canada

Money in Other Countries

Every country in the world has its own money. The money in each country is different.

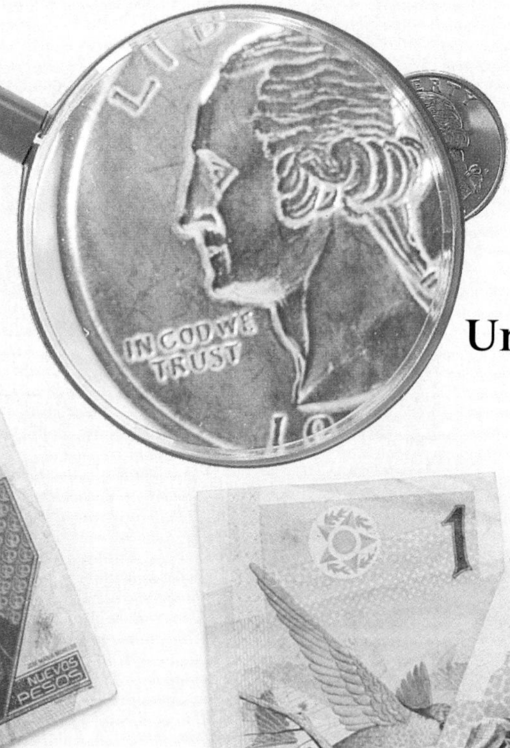

United States

Mexico

Brazil

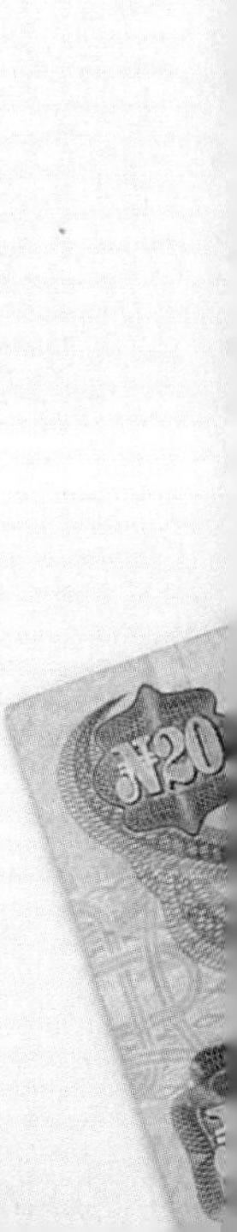

92

France

Japan

England

In the United States we have paper money
called dollars. Paper money has different
names in other countries. In England they
have pounds. In Mexico they have pesos.

?

1. What is paper money in England called?

2. Into what two groups could you sort the
   money on these pages?

Australia

Nigeria

Using Picture Graphs

A **picture graph** uses picture symbols to show numbers of things. The title tells you what the picture graph shows. This picture graph shows Pam's coins. Each picture symbol stands for one coin.

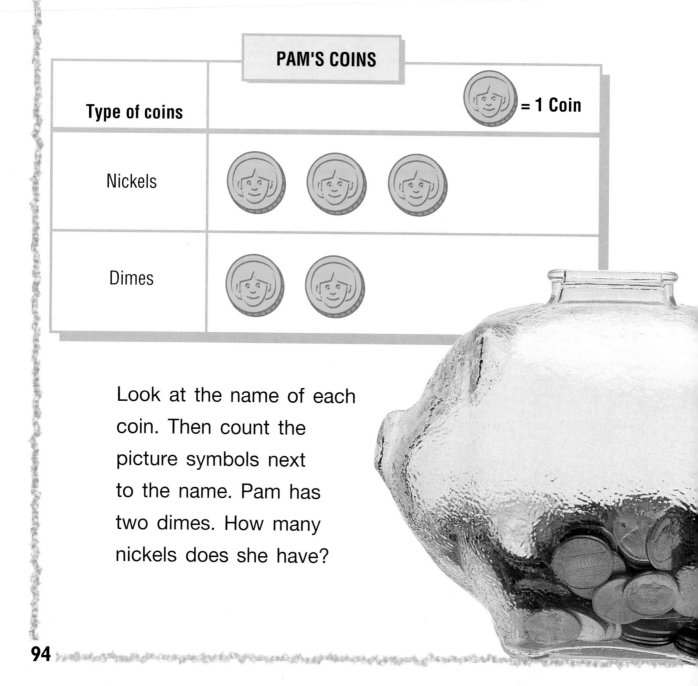

PAM'S COINS

Type of coins		= 1 Coin
Nickels		
Dimes		

Look at the name of each coin. Then count the picture symbols next to the name. Pam has two dimes. How many nickels does she have?

Trying the Skill

Pam also has some money from other countries. Use this picture graph to answer the questions about her coins.

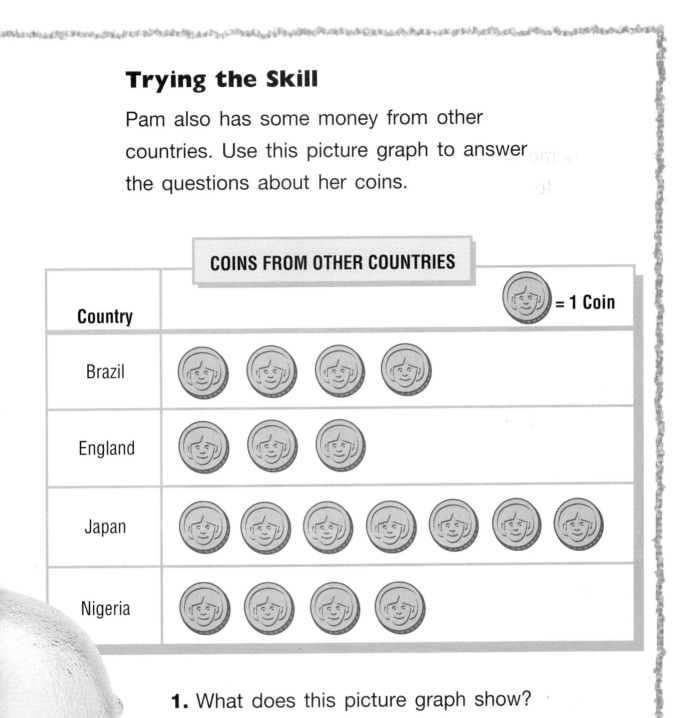

COINS FROM OTHER COUNTRIES

= 1 Coin

Country	
Brazil	😊 😊 😊 😊
England	😊 😊 😊
Japan	😊 😊 😊 😊 😊 😊 😊
Nigeria	😊 😊 😊 😊

1. What does this picture graph show?
2. How many coins from England does Pam have?
3. Does Pam have more coins from Japan or from Brazil? How did you figure this out?

Money's

Funny

by Mary Ann Hoberman

Money's funny
Don't you think?
Nickel's bigger than a dime;
So's a cent;
But when they're spent,
Dime is worth more
Every time.

Money's funny.

UNIT 3 REVIEW

Thinking About Words

Tell if these sentences are true or false. If
the sentence is false, tell how to make it true.

1. **Wants** are the same for all people.
2. A place to live is called a **shelter**.
3. Things that are made or grown are **goods**.
4. **Needs** are things people can do without.
5. **Transportation** is how people or things
   move from one place to another.
6. A **service** is work done for others.
7. **Volunteers** are paid for their work.
8. A **job** is work that people do.

Thinking About Ideas

1. Why do people work?
2. What are four needs all people have?
3. Name some ways people help in your community.
4. Tell two ways that United States money
   is like money in other countries.

What job would you like to do
when you grow up? Tell why.

Using Skills

Reviewing Using Picture Graphs

1. What does this picture graph show?
2. How many people work in an office?
3. How many people work in a store?
4. Where do most of the people work?

Where People In Our Families Work		🧍 Stands For One Worker
Factory	🧍 🧍 🧍 🧍 🧍 🧍	
Store	🧍 🧍 🧍 🧍 🧍	
Office	🧍 🧍 🧍 🧍	

Make Your Own!

- Make a picture graph. Show how many times you helped at home this week.
- List three jobs on the side of the graph.
- Draw a symbol of a house to show each time you helped.

Using Skills

Reviewing Sorting Things into Groups

Use these pictures to answer the questions about sorting.

1. Sort these pictures into two groups

2. How are the things in each group alike?

3. How are the two groups different?

4. What other things could you add to each group?

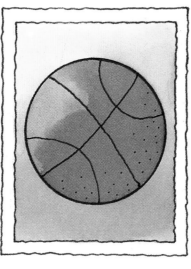

UNIT PROJECT

Make a Neighborhood of Shops

- Choose a store to make.
- Use a piece of paper to make windows. Glue them to a shoe box.
- Draw or cut out pictures that show goods or services in your store.
- Make a sign for your store.

Reading on Your Own

You can look for these books at your library.

UNIT FOUR

Our World

Key Words

plain

hill

mountain

lake

river

ocean

weather

season

continent

natural resource

Our Land and Water

Suppose you were flying high above the United States on a kite. You would see many kinds of land and bodies of water.

Let's look at different kinds of land. This flat land is called a **plain**. Most plains are good for farming. This plain is in the state of Wisconsin.

These **hills** are in California. A hill is land that is higher than the land around it. People camp and hike in these hills.

Mountains are the highest kind of land. This is Mount McKinley in Alaska. It is the tallest mountain in our country.

Now let's look at bodies of water. A **lake** is a body of water. It has land all around it. The city of Chicago is by Lake Michigan. Lakes can be big or small.

A **river** is a long body of water that flows across the land. This is a river in North Dakota.

Some rivers flow into lakes. Other rivers flow into **oceans**. An ocean is a very big body of salt water. This is the Atlantic Ocean. Some of the food we eat comes from this ocean.

1. Sort <u>plain</u>, <u>river</u>, <u>mountain</u>, and <u>lake</u> into two groups.

2. How are lakes and rivers different?

GEOGRAPHY SKILLS
Using Directions

North, east, south, and west are four **directions** on Earth. These directions can help you to find places on maps.

North is the direction toward the North Pole. South is the direction toward the South Pole. When you face north, east is to your right. What direction is to your left?

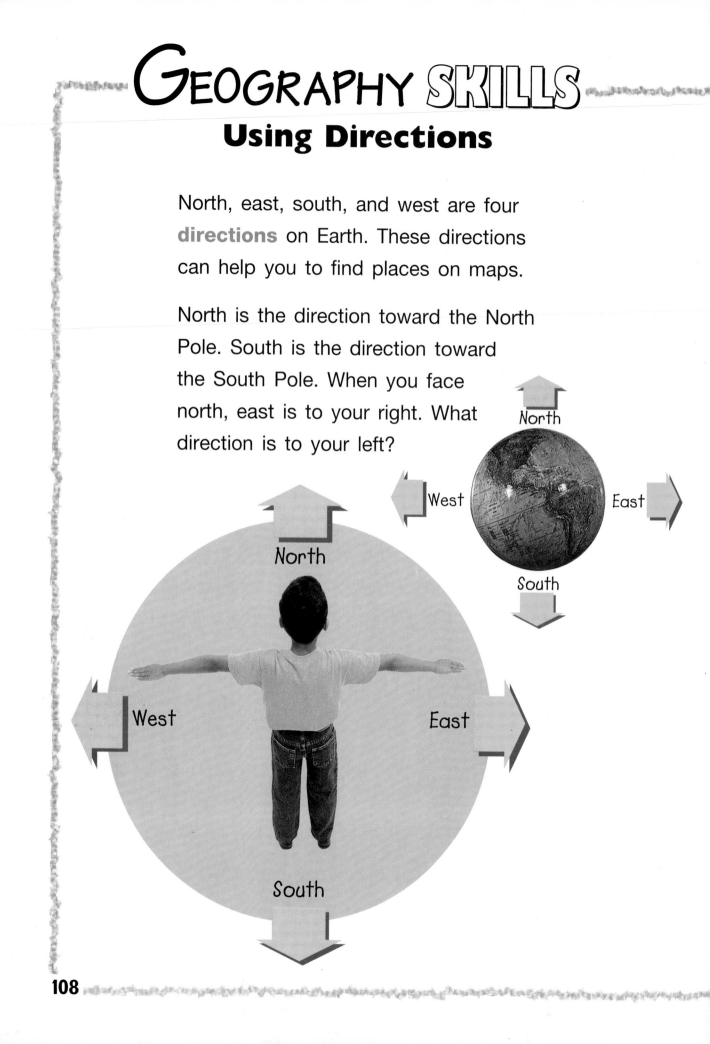

Trying the Skill

Use the map of the state of Kentucky to answer the questions below.

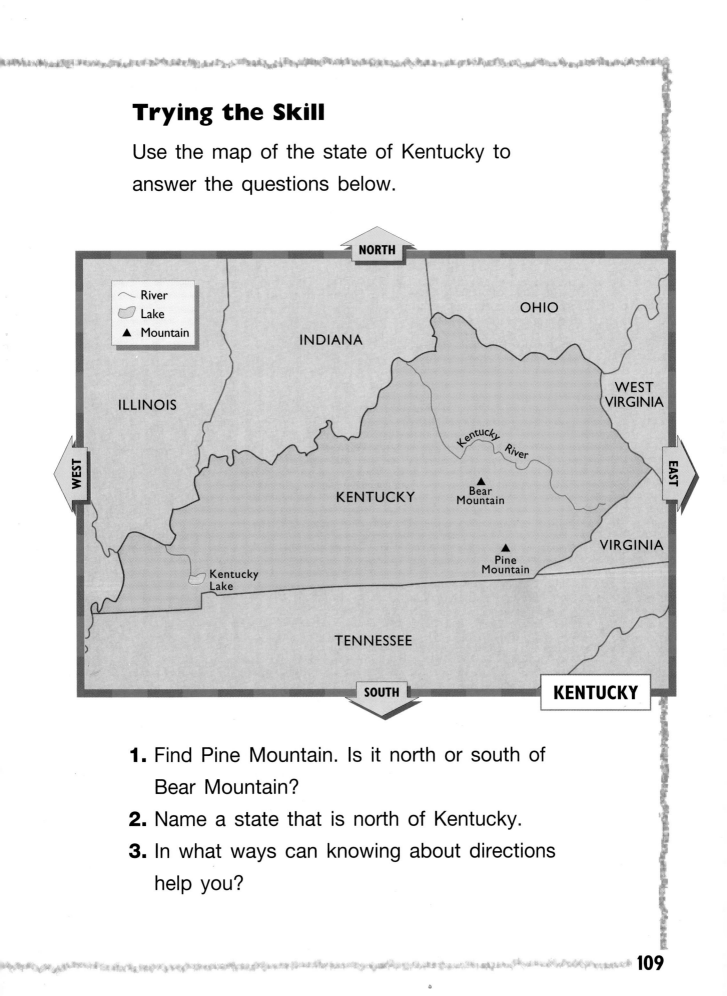

1. Find Pine Mountain. Is it north or south of Bear Mountain?
2. Name a state that is north of Kentucky.
3. In what ways can knowing about directions help you?

How's the Weather?

Beth lives in Indiana. Matt lives in California. Beth wanted to know if both states have the same **weather**. Weather is what it is like outside. Read their letters. What did Beth find out?

Dear Matt,

Yesterday it rained. Then it started to snow. It snowed all night. The sun is out today, but it is cold. I made this snowman. Did you get lots of snow in California too?

Your friend,
Beth

Dear Beth,

It rained here on the day you got snow. The sun came out the next day. It was warm and windy. Dad took me to the beach. Here is a sandman I made. I liked your snowman a lot!

Your friend,
Matt

Beth found out that two places can have different weather at the same time. Some places in the North might be cold. On the same day, some places in the South might be warm.

In many places the weather changes as the **seasons** change. The seasons are spring, summer, fall, and winter. Here is what the seasons are like where Beth lives.

Summer

Spring

Winter

Fall

How do trees change as the
seasons change?

1. Use the words <u>yesterday</u>, <u>today</u>, and
   <u>tomorrow</u> to tell about your weather.

2. Tell about the seasons where you live.
   How are they like Beth's? How are
   they different?

113

THINKING SKILLS
Putting Things in Order

When you put things in **order**, you tell what comes first, next, and last. You can put things in order by size or by time.

These pictures are in order by time. The first picture shows a clay ball. What does the next picture show? The last picture shows a clay snowman.

Trying the Skill

Put the pictures below in order.

1. Which picture comes first?
2. Which picture comes next?
3. Which picture comes last?
4. How does putting these pictures in order help to tell a story?

a.

b.

c.

Our Neighbors, Canada and Mexico

The United States has a neighbor country to the north. This country is Canada. Mexico is our neighbor to the south.

NORTH

ALASKA (U.S.)

CANADA

WEST

EAST

UNITED STATES

PACIFIC OCEAN

ATLANTIC OCEAN

MEXICO

SOUTH

THE UNITED STATES AND ITS NEIGHBORS

Taqtu lives in Canada. The winters are cold and snowy there. The summers are warm.

Carlos lives in Mexico. The weather there is warm and sunny most of the year.

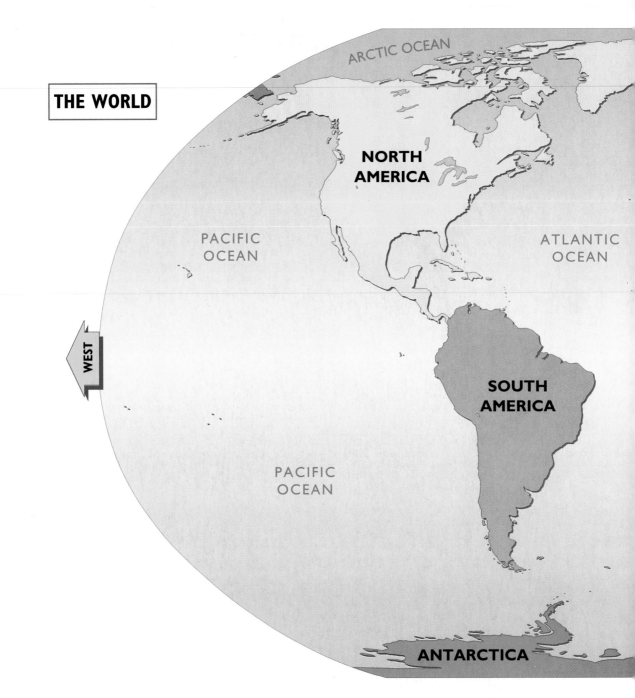

THE WORLD

ARCTIC OCEAN

NORTH AMERICA

PACIFIC OCEAN

ATLANTIC OCEAN

WEST

SOUTH AMERICA

PACIFIC OCEAN

ANTARCTICA

The United States and its neighbor countries are part of North America. North America is a **continent**. A continent is one of seven large bodies of land on Earth. What is the name of the continent south of North America?

Oceans are the large bodies of water around the continents. Name the four oceans on Earth.

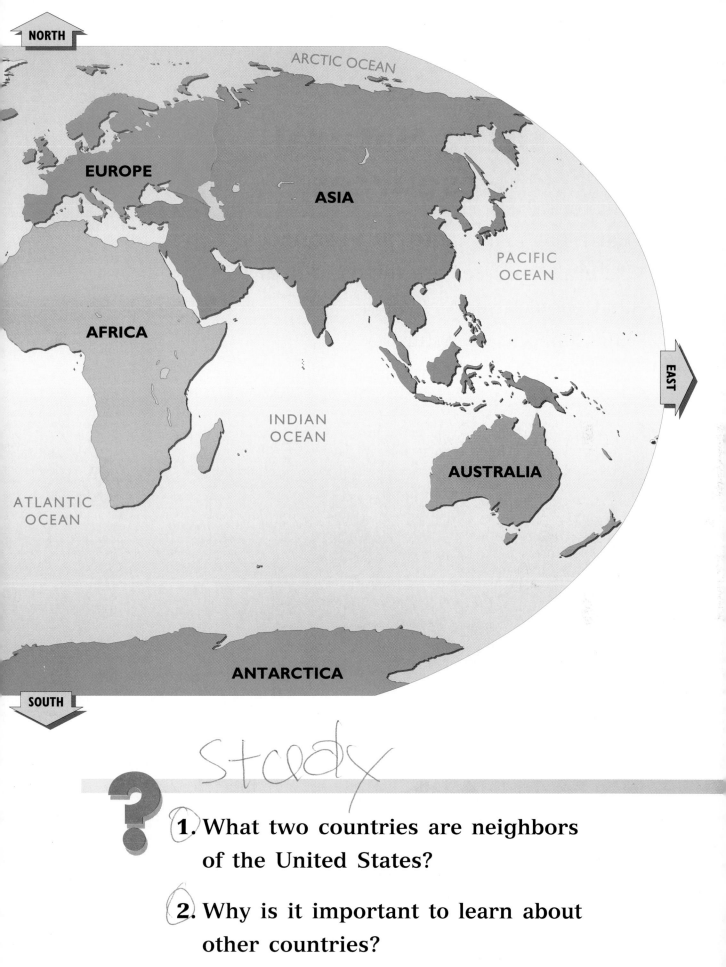

NORTH

ARCTIC OCEAN

EUROPE

ASIA

PACIFIC OCEAN

AFRICA

EAST

INDIAN OCEAN

AUSTRALIA

ATLANTIC OCEAN

ANTARCTICA

SOUTH

steady

?

1. What two countries are neighbors of the United States?

2. Why is it important to learn about other countries?

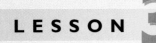

Using Natural Resources

Earth has many **natural resources**. Natural resources are things in nature that people use. Air, water, and sunlight are natural resources. We need these resources to live.

Animals, plants, and soil are natural resources too. We use them to make food and other goods. Natural resources like coal, oil, and gas come from under the ground. They warm our homes.

Trees are another natural resource. They help store water in the ground. They keep the air clean. They give us food too. Many things we use are made from trees. Can you name anything made from trees?

Everyone needs clean water to drink. Here are other ways people use this natural resource.

1. What are three natural resources you use?

2. In what ways are natural resources important to us?

Caring for Our Natural Resources

"Welcome to Chain O'Lakes State Park," says Miss Hart. She is showing Beth's class around the park. This park is in Indiana.

"A state park is a special place," says Miss Hart. "People come here to enjoy the trees, fresh air, and other natural resources."

"It is important to take care of Earth's natural resources. If we use them up, we won't have any left," says Miss Hart.

Here are some things you can do to
help care for our Earth.

Help animals.

Keep our land, air, and
water clean and beautiful.

Save things like these.
They can be made
into something new.

Use things over
and over.

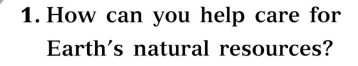

1. How can you help care for
   Earth's natural resources?

2. What might happen if we
   don't take care of our
   natural resources?

127

CITIZENSHIP
Making a Difference

CALIFORNIA

Los Angeles

Earth Niños

Yvette Ugalde wants Earth to be a clean place with lots of trees. She joined a club to help make this happen. The name of the club is Earth Niños. These English and Spanish words mean "Children for the Earth." The club is at the Humphreys Avenue School in Los Angeles, California.

Yvette and other children in the club collect empty cans. Then the children wash each can and squash it flat.

128

Ralph Sanders is the teacher who started the club. He takes the cans to a place where they can be reused. The club gets paid a little money for each can. Then they use the money to buy trees for the schoolyard.

So far the Earth Niños club has bought and planted 50 trees. Yvette says, "I feel happy because we are making the earth feel better."

from

IT'S MY EARTH, TOO

HOW I CAN HELP THE
EARTH STAY ALIVE

BY
KATHLEEN KRULL

ILLUSTRATED BY
MELANIE HOPE GREENBERG

It's my Earth, too—
The Earth is where I live.
It gives me air to breathe,
water to drink,
soil for growing my food,
and animals to play with.
It's my Earth, too.

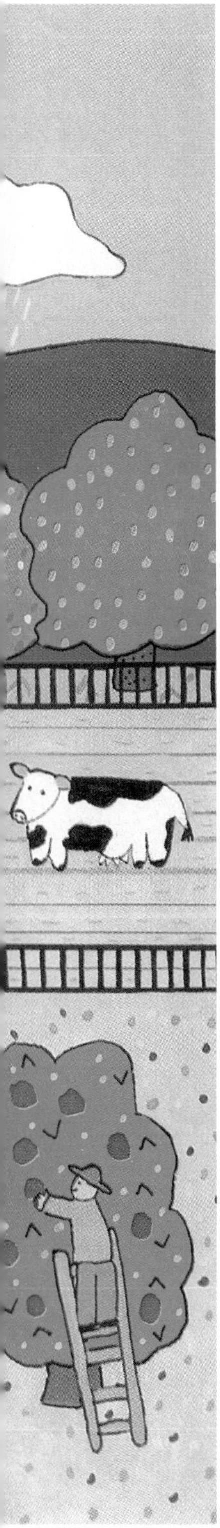

Oranges are juicy.

Carrots are crunchy.

Lettuce is munchy.

To get this food from the Earth to my stomach

takes rays of sunshine,

clean air blowing,

streams of rain,

and mounds of good soil.

That's a lot of the Earth's energy.

Shhhh—leaves whisper way above my head.
Squirrels run up and down the tall trees.
I wonder just how paper is made from trees.
The paper things I use every day
come from trees just like these.

Splish, splash. Water in my bath.

Drip, drop. Water from the faucet.

Water in the drinking fountain.

Hurray for water!

Without it we'd be always dirty, sticky, and thirsty.

That would make us crabby, mean, and sick.

It's my Earth, too.

I hope that the air and water are always clean,

that the soil is always good,

that the animals stay alive,

that there is plenty of everything to go around.

UNIT 4 REVIEW

Thinking About Words

Match the words with the sentences below.

plain	hill		mountain	lake
river	ocean		weather	season
continents	natural resources			

1. I am the highest kind of land.
2. I am flat land.
3. I am a big body of salt water.
4. I am water surrounded by land.
5. We are trees, air, water, and sunlight.
6. There are seven of us on Earth.
7. I flow across the land.
8. I am not flat land or very high land.
9. I am spring, summer, fall, or winter.
10. I can be hot, cold, sunny, snowy, or rainy.

Thinking About Ideas

1. Tell how a river and an ocean are different.
2. What land and water are near you?
3. Tell how each season is different.

Tell about ways you can care for natural resources at school.

138

Using Skills

Reviewing Using Directions

Use the map to answer these questions.

1. Is Crater Lake to the north or south of Columbia River?
2. In what part of Oregon is the Powder River?
3. Are the Blue Mountains to the east or west of Crater Lake?

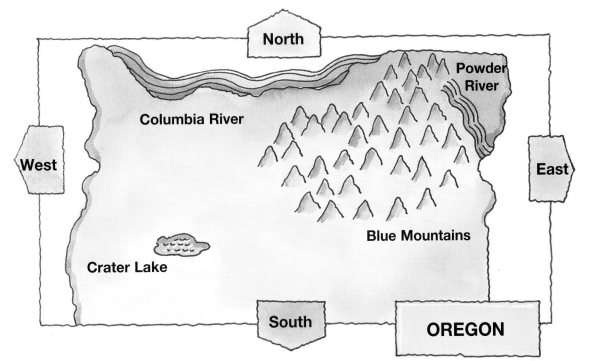

Make Your Own!

- Write each of the four directions on a different card.
- Tape the direction cards to your desk.
- Use the directions to tell where things are in your classroom.

Using Skills

Reviewing Putting Things in Order

Put these pictures in order.

1. Which picture comes first?

2. Which picture comes next?

3. Which picture comes last?

4. How does putting these pictures in order help to tell a story?

a.

b.

c.

Make a Poster of Resources

- Draw pictures of natural resources, such as sun, water, and trees.
- Choose one of these natural resources. Make a poster to show how this natural resource is used.
- Write the name of the natural resource on the poster.

Reading on Your Own

You can look for these books at your library.

It Happened in America

Key Words

history

time line

Native Americans

settler

settlement

Pilgrims

Learning About the Past

What do you know about your past?
Read this story about Kevin. You
will see how he learned about
his past.

My grandma has a quilt. It has patches
in all the colors of the rainbow. One
day I saw Grandma looking at the quilt.
I wondered what she was thinking.

"Each patch in the quilt tells about the
past," Grandma told me.

"The white patch is from my wedding gown. I love to look at it. It helps me remember the day I married your grandfather."

"The red patch is from a baseball cap. It was your Dad's cap when he was a boy," she said.

"What about me?" I asked. "Is there a patch that tells about my past?"

"There sure is," she said. "This blue patch is a piece of your first blanket. It's six years old, just like you!"

Now when I look at Grandma's quilt, I remember the stories about my family's past.

Kevin learned about his family's past from a quilt. Our country has a past too. This past is called our **history**.

There are many ways to learn about our country's history. What ways do these pictures show?

1. What are some ways people learn about their past?

2. How can we learn about our country's history?

STUDY SKILLS

Using Time Lines

A **time line** shows the order of things that happened. This time line shows what Kevin's grandmother did in one week. Each box on the time line is one day.

Sunday	Monday	Tuesday	Wednesday	Thursday	Friday	Saturday

Planted roses	Added patches to quilt	Worked at the library	Went shopping	Worked at the library	Celebrated Kevin's birthday	Went to zoo with Kevin

The time line starts on Sunday. On that day Kevin's grandmother planted roses. On Monday she added patches to her quilt. What did she do on Friday?

Trying the Skill

This time line tells about things that happened in Kevin's past. Each box on the time line is one year.

1 year old	2 years old	3 years old	4 years old	5 years old	6 years old
Learned to walk	Sister Jennie born	Learned to ride a bike	Learned to write name	Started school	Lost first tooth

Use the time line to answer these questions.

1. When did Kevin start to walk?

2. What happened when he was 2 years old?

3. How old was Kevin when he started school?

4. How would a time line help you remember events in your life?

The First People in America

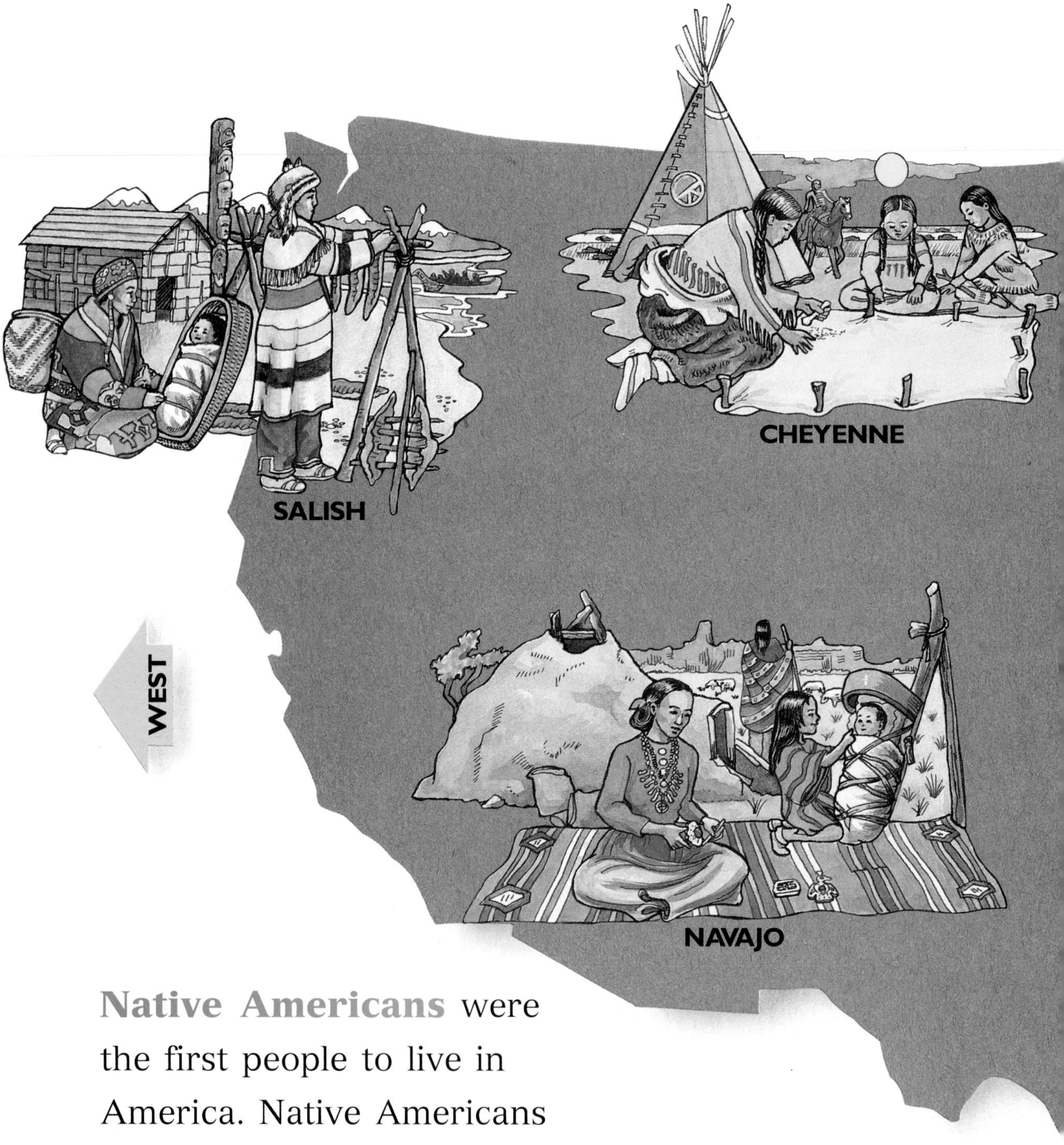

CHEYENNE

SALISH

WEST

NAVAJO

Native Americans were
the first people to live in
America. Native Americans
are also called Indians.

There are many different groups of Native Americans. This map shows where some lived long ago. Today some Native Americans live in the same places. Find the Navajo on the map.

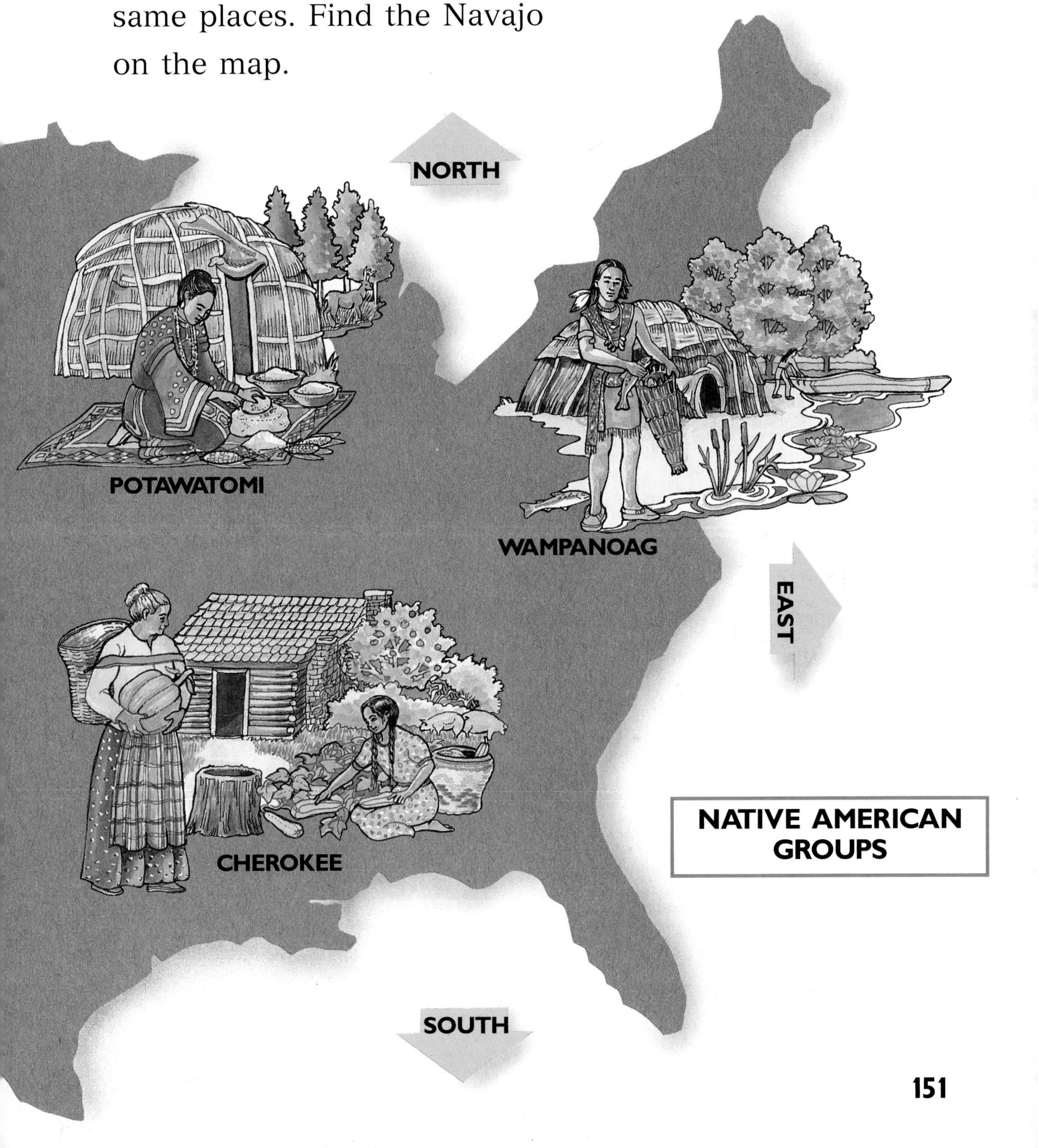

NORTH

POTAWATOMI

WAMPANOAG

EAST

CHEROKEE

NATIVE AMERICAN GROUPS

SOUTH

Deirdra's Scrapbook

my teacher

↑
me

My name is Deirdra. I am
Navajo. We call ourselves
Diné. *Diné* means "the people"
in our language.

Arizona

My family lives in the state of Arizona.
I am learning about Navajo history. I am
learning from my family and my teacher.

In the past Navajo families lived in hogans. Hogans were one-room houses. They were made of logs, tree bark, and mud.

bark↗

sheep →

Navajo families raised sheep. The sheep were used for food and wool. The wool made beautiful blankets and cloth.

Look at these pictures. They show my community today.

Some Navajo still live in hogans. We still do many things as in the past. I like knowing that the Navajo have a special history.

1. **Who were the first people to live in America?**

2. **Why do you think Deirdra wants to learn about Navajo history?**

Christopher Columbus Comes to America

"Land! Land!" a sailor called out to his captain. The captain was Christopher Columbus.

The Granger Collection

Columbus and his crew sailed across the Atlantic Ocean over 500 years ago. They sailed from Spain. Spain is a country in Europe.

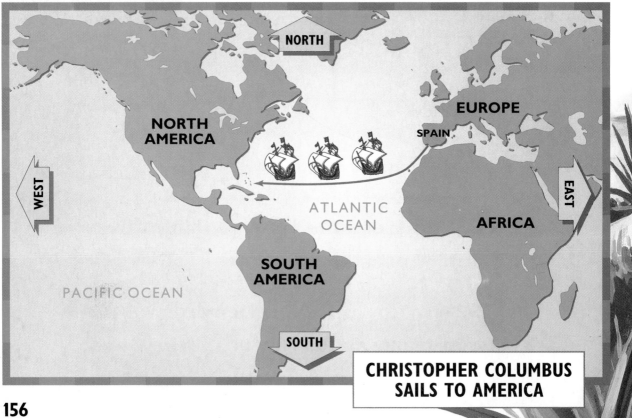

NORTH

EUROPE

NORTH AMERICA

SPAIN

WEST

EAST

ATLANTIC OCEAN

AFRICA

SOUTH AMERICA

PACIFIC OCEAN

SOUTH

CHRISTOPHER COLUMBUS SAILS TO AMERICA

Columbus's ships were named the *Niña,* the *Pinta,* and the *Santa María.* Columbus had hoped to find gold and riches in Asia. Instead he landed on an island in North America.

Native Americans called the Taino lived on the island. The Taino welcomed Columbus and his men.

The Taino brought the sailors plants and birds that lived on their island. They also gave them tomatoes and corn. The sailors had never seen these foods before.

Columbus returned to Spain. He took back the birds and plants that the Taino gave him.

Columbus made three more trips to North America. He never found much gold. But he did find a place that people in Europe did not know about.

1. Who lived on the island where Columbus landed?

2. Why do you think Columbus took birds and plants back to Spain?

STUDY SKILLS
Finding the Main Idea

The **main idea** tells what a story is about. Finding the main idea helps you to understand what you read.

Read this story to find the main idea.

Christopher Columbus wanted to learn about the world. He became a good sailor. He studied maps. He asked fishermen and sailors about the places they had been.

Sometimes the main idea of a story is the first sentence. The main idea in this story is that Christopher Columbus wanted to learn about the world. The other sentences tell what he did to learn about the world.

Trying the Skill

Read this story to find the main idea.

The Taino were good boat builders. They built large boats called canoes. The Taino sailed many miles in their canoes. Some Taino canoes could hold 100 people.

1. What is the main idea of this story?

2. How can knowing the main idea be helpful?

A Place Called Santa Fe

People from many countries came to North America after Columbus. These people were called **settlers**. Settlers are people who move from one place to live in a different place.

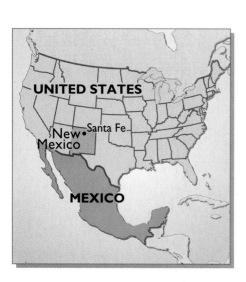

Settlers from Spain moved north from Mexico. Some settled on land that is now the state of New Mexico. They started new **settlements**. A settlement is a small community. One settlement became Santa Fe.

162

Native Americans lived nearby. The Spanish called them "Pueblos." Their homes were called pueblos too.

Today Santa Fe is one of the oldest cities in America. There are still pueblos nearby. You can see some of these places built long ago.

Visiting a pueblo

1. What is a settler?

2. What places in your community were built long ago?

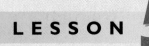
Pilgrims at Plymouth

Later another group of settlers came to North America. These people were called **Pilgrims**. They left their homes in England to start a new life.

The Pilgrims crossed the Atlantic Ocean in a ship called the *Mayflower*. In America they hoped they could pray to God as they wished.

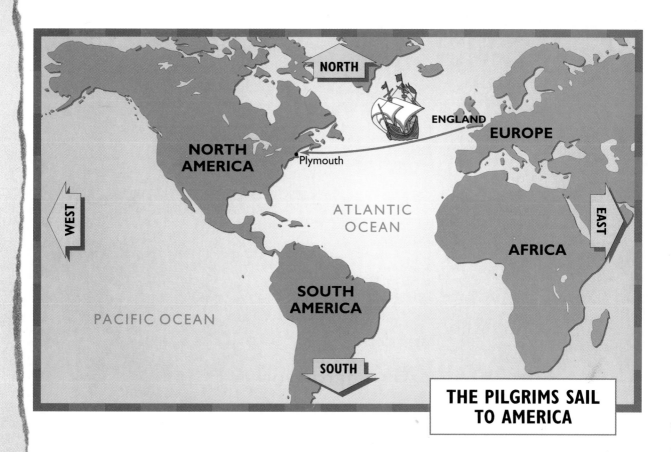

NORTH

ENGLAND

EUROPE

NORTH
AMERICA

Plymouth

WEST

EAST

ATLANTIC
OCEAN

AFRICA

SOUTH
AMERICA

PACIFIC OCEAN

SOUTH

**THE PILGRIMS SAIL
TO AMERICA**

The trip was hard for the Pilgrims.
There were storms at sea. Many people
became sick.

One day the Pilgrims finally heard "Land
Ho!" They had reached America. It was
winter and very cold.

The Pilgrims were hard workers. They began to build a town called Plymouth.

In the spring the Pilgrims met the Wampanoag Indians. They lived near the Pilgrims.

The Wampanoag sent Squanto to help the Pilgrims. Squanto showed the Pilgrims how to fish, hunt, and plant corn.

By fall the fields were full of corn. The Pilgrims decided to have a feast. They asked the Native Americans to come.

The Pilgrims gave thanks to God. They had enough food, strong homes, and good friends.

Now at Thanksgiving, we remember the Pilgrims and the Native Americans who helped them.

1. How did Squanto help the Pilgrims?

2. How is Thanksgiving today like the Pilgrims' Thanksgiving?

A Country of Many People

More and more people came to America. They came from many countries in Europe.

People came to start a new life. Many people came to America to pray to God in their own way. They wanted to be free.

Baltimore Historical Society

The Granger Collection

Some people did not come to America by their own choice. These people were from Africa. Many Africans were made to come to America as slaves. They had to work without pay.

The people from Africa dreamed of being free one day. That day came after a long time.

As many new people moved to America they built homes and farms. They raised families. They worked in shops and schools. They built places to pray.

Towns and cities grew. Soon there was a new country. This country became the United States of America.

The Granger Collection

Sam Mar Dock was born in China.
He and many other people from
China worked to build the railroads.
The railroads crossed the country as
the United States grew larger.

A boy named Edward Corsi was 10 years
old when he came to the United States.
His family came from Italy by boat.

The first thing Edward saw was the Statue
of Liberty. He remembers that mothers
and fathers held their babies high to show
them the statue. The United States was the
country of their dreams.

Today people are still coming to the United States. They come from many countries around the world.

The United States is still the land of dreams.

1. Tell reasons why people came to America long ago.

2. Why do you think people come to the United States today?

CITIZENSHIP
Making a Difference

NEW YORK

New York City

Miss Janey and class

Welcome to New York City

Janey Markon is a teacher in New York City. She and other teachers work with "Project Reach Youth." They help children from all over the world who move to New York City.

"Miss Janey" knows that moving to a new place is not easy. There is so much to learn. "Moving to the United States can seem like moving to a different planet," says Miss Janey.

Taking the bus

Jelen

Miss Janey teaches the children English. She also shows them how to use money and how to get around on a bus.

Miss Janey thinks that doing things in the city is very important. She says, "The more that children know about a new place, the sooner they will feel at home."

Jelen DeCastro is from the Dominican Republic. He loves New York pizza!

WHAT WAS

"What was it like
when you were as old as I am now?"
a little girl asked her mother.
"Well, when I went to bed,"
her mother said,
"the room was dark
the clocks ticked
grown-ups talked downstairs
the stars shone in the sky
and I could hear the wind in the trees
   outside
before I hugged my mother good night
the way you do now."

BY CHARLOTTE ZOLOTOW
ILLUSTRATED BY MELISSA SWEET

UNIT 5 REVIEW

Thinking About Words

Choose the word or words that best tell about each sentence.

| history | Pilgrims | settlers | settlement |
| Native Americans |

1. These people are also called Indians.
2. This is a small community built by settlers.
3. These are people who move from one place to live in a different place.
4. This is our country's past.
5. These people came to North America on the *Mayflower*.

Thinking About Ideas

1. Who were the first Americans?
2. How did North America change after Columbus came here?
3. Why did the Pilgrims have a feast?
4. Why did people come to America long ago?

What is your favorite story from our country's past? Tell why.

Using Skills

Reviewing Using Time Lines

This time line tells about the Pilgrims' first year in America.

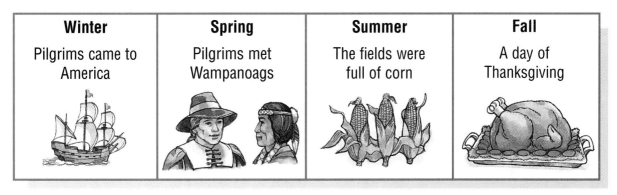

Winter	Spring	Summer	Fall
Pilgrims came to America	Pilgrims met Wampanoags	The fields were full of corn	A day of Thanksgiving

1. What happened in the fall?

2. What happened in the spring?

3. When did the Pilgrims come to America?

Make Your Own!

- Write each day of the week at the top of a different sheet of paper.
- Draw what you did that day.
- Put pictures in order. Start with Sunday.
- Tape your pictures together.

Using Skills

Reviewing Finding the Main Idea

Read this story to find the main idea.

People from many places built communities in America. They built homes and farms. They worked in schools. They built railroads.

1. What is the main idea of this story?

2. Which three pictures tell about the main idea?

3. Which picture does not show the main idea? Why?

a.

b.

c.

d.

UNIT PROJECT

Make a History Storybook

- Choose a person or group from history, such as Native Americans or Pilgrims.
- Draw three pictures of the person or group.
- Write a sentence under each picture.
- Punch a hole in each page.
- Tie your book together with a piece of yarn.

Reading on Your Own

You can look for these books at your library.

UNIT SIX

Americans Celebrate

Key Words

holiday

calendar

celebrate

Holidays for Presidents

Holidays are special days. On some holidays we remember important people. On others we remember something that happened.

Presidents' Day is a holiday in February. On Presidents' Day we remember George Washington.

George Washington

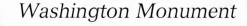

George Washington's Home

Washington Monument

Long ago America was not free. It was ruled by the country of England.

Americans fought a war to become free. George Washington was our leader. Later he became our first President. He is called the "Father of our Country."

Abraham Lincoln was President long after George Washington. When Lincoln was a child, he was poor. He worked hard to become a leader.

President Lincoln worked to keep our country together during a war. He helped to free African Americans from slavery.

Abraham Lincoln

On Presidents' Day we remember Abraham Lincoln too. We remember him as a strong leader. We remember him as fair. He is called "Honest Abe."

Abraham Lincoln's Home

Lincoln Memorial

1. Who do we remember on Presidents' Day?

2. How are George Washington and Abraham Lincoln alike?

STUDY SKILLS
Using Calendars

Calendars are charts that show the months of a year. They show the weeks in a month. They also show the days in a week. Calendars show holidays too.

This calendar shows the month of February. Each block on the calendar is one day. How many days are in this month? February 14 is a Friday. What is the name of that day?

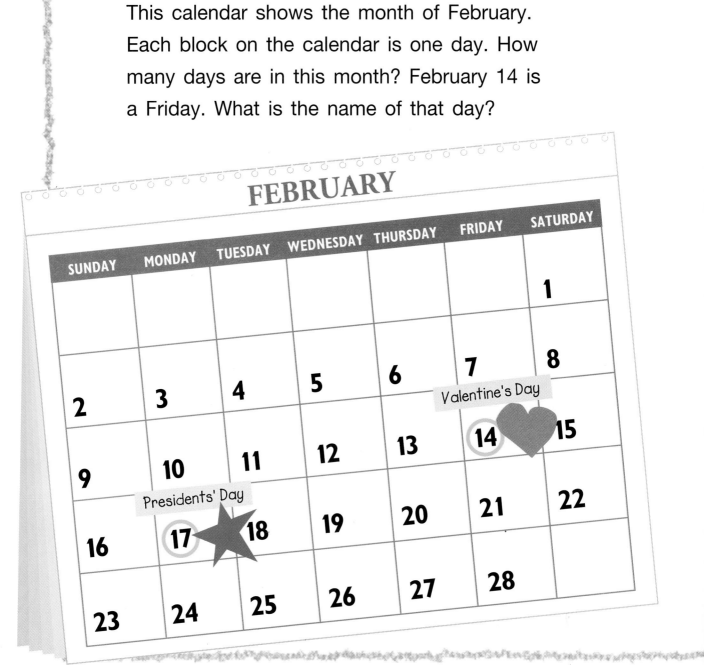

JUNE

SUNDAY	MONDAY	TUESDAY	WEDNESDAY	THURSDAY	FRIDAY	SATURDAY
1	2	3	4	5	6	7
8	9	10	11	12	13	**14** Flag Day
15 Father's Day	16	17	18	19	20	21
22	23	24	25	26	27	28
29	30					

Trying the Skill

Use the calendar above to answer these questions.

1. How many days are in this month?

2. What day of the week is June 14? What is the name of that day?

3. On which day is Father's Day?

4. How is a calendar useful?

Special Days for Our Country

Americans **celebrate** many holidays.
We celebrate by doing something special.
What holidays can you name?

We celebrate Independence Day on July 4.
We remember July 4 in 1776. On that day
the United States said it was free
from England. People cheered.
Bells rang. Cannons boomed!

Independence Day is our country's birthday. We celebrate with parades and fireworks. We show that we are proud to be Americans.

JULY

Columbus Day is in October. On that day we remember when Christopher Columbus came to America.

Thanksgiving Day is in November. We remember the feast shared by the Pilgrims and the Native Americans. Today we still celebrate with a big dinner. We also give thanks.

In January we remember Martin Luther King, Jr. He worked to make laws fair for all Americans. He had a dream that all people will get along. We remember his dream.

JANUARY

The Kansas City, Kansas
Martin Luther King Jr.
Holiday Celebration Committee
His Dream Lives On

?

1. Name two holidays for our country. Why do we celebrate them?

2. Why do people celebrate holidays?

THINKING SKILLS
Making Predictions

When you tell what you think will happen next, you are making a **prediction**. Read the story below. This story is about our country's flag. Make a prediction about what will happen next.

Betsy Ross liked to sew. She made clothes. President George Washington wanted a flag for our new country. He knew Betsy Ross could sew.

What do you think George Washington did? Did you make the prediction that George Washington asked Betsy Ross to make our flag? If so, you are right!

Trying the Skill

Read the story below. Then answer the questions.

Betsy Ross cut out the pieces to make a flag. She sewed the red and white stripes together. She sewed on the stars. Then George Washington came to see the flag.

1. What do you think happened next? Tell the reasons for your prediction.
2. How does making predictions help you in school?

Special Days for Families

Families celebrate many special days.

They celebrate the day a new baby is born.

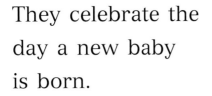

Families also celebrate when a child finishes school.

196

A wedding is another special day. We celebrate when a man and a woman get married. They become a new family.

Sometimes all the members of a family get together. This is a way to remember the past.

Reunion

Some families share other special days too.
These holidays are celebrated every year.

Christmas is celebrated
on December 25.

Hanukkah is usually
celebrated in December.
It lasts eight days.

Kwanzaa begins on December 26.
It ends on January 6.

Chinese New Year is celebrated in January or February. The holiday lasts three days.

Three Kings Day is celebrated on January 6.

1. Do all families celebrate the same special days? Tell why or why not.

2. How will you celebrate your next special day? Make a prediction.

Celebrating with Pictures

Medford Cole has a picture of a shiny red car. It hangs on the wall of his home in Houston, Texas. He took the picture himself.

His sister Audreaya takes pictures too. Her favorite ones show family celebrations. "My very best pictures are from my birthday party," she says. "I took pictures of everyone eating cake."

TEXAS

Houston

Audreaya's birthday party

Audreaya taking pictures

Medford and Audreaya learned to take pictures at a program called Project Bridge. Their teacher is Karen Sanders.

The children get cameras and film to take home. They take pictures of their neighborhood and their families. These pictures help them to remember special days.

Miss Sanders picks some of the best pictures for a children's photography show. The children invite their families and friends to come. "I felt so good when I saw my pictures at that show," says Medford.

Celebrating Spring

People in many places around the world celebrate the start of spring.

In the United States, some children roll Easter eggs on the White House lawn.

People in China celebrate with a holiday called Ching Ming. People clean house, plant flowers, and remember their families.

On the first day in May, children in England sing and dance around the Maypole. They are celebrating trees in spring.

In Spain people go to a Spring Fair. They put up tents for parties. They ride in parades on horses.

1. What are two ways people celebrate spring?

2. Why do you think people in many places like to celebrate spring?

Symbols Say U.S.A.!

Many symbols stand for the United States. These symbols remind us of our country.

The Statue of Liberty is a symbol. It stands for hope. It also stands for freedom and friendship. This statue is in New York Harbor. It welcomes new people to our country.

The Liberty Bell is a symbol. It stands for freedom. It was rung when the United States became a country. The bell has a big crack. So it can no longer ring. You can see this symbol in the city of Philadelphia, Pennsylvania.

The bald eagle is another symbol. It stands for our country. This symbol is shown on some of our country's money.

The American flag is an important symbol of our country. It has 13 stripes and 50 stars. Each star stands for a state. The flag is red, white, and blue.

white

CRAYON

THE PLEDGE OF ALLEGIANCE

I pledge allegiance to the flag of the United States of America and to the Republic for which it stands, one Nation under God, indivisible, with liberty and justice for all.

We say the *Pledge of Allegiance*. It honors our flag and our country. We honor our flag on Flag Day, June 14.

?

1. Name two symbols of the United States.

2. Why do you think we have symbols for our country?

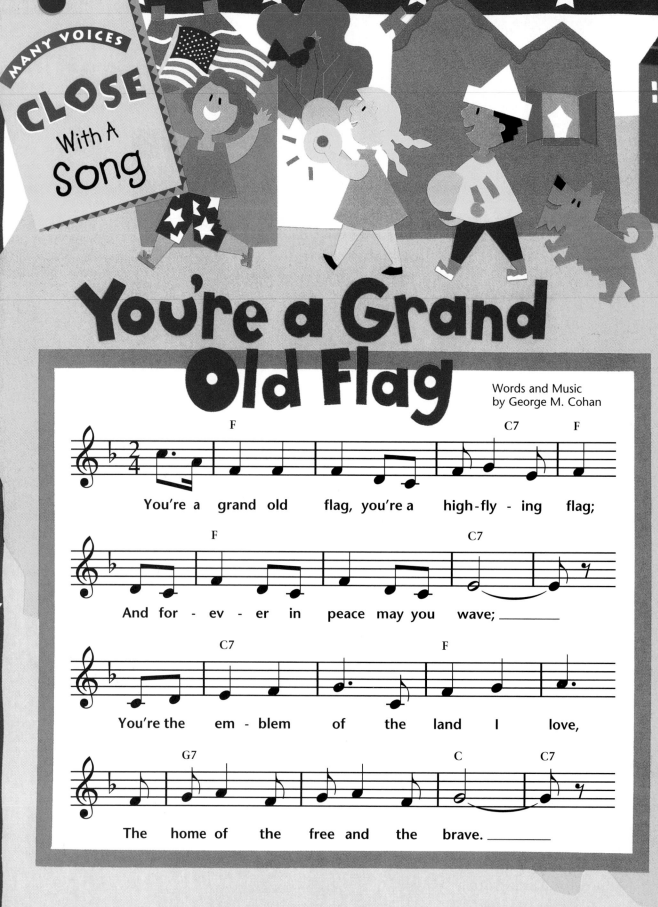

You're a Grand Old Flag

Words and Music
by George M. Cohan

You're a grand old flag, you're a high-fly-ing flag;

And for-ev-er in peace may you wave; _____

You're the em-blem of the land I love,

The home of the free and the brave. _____

UNIT 6 REVIEW

Thinking About Words

Use these words to finish the sentences.

calendar	holiday	celebrate
prediction		

1. A special day is a _____.
2. A _____ is a chart that shows the days, weeks, and months of the year.
3. Americans _____ many holidays each year.
4. You make a _____ when you tell what you think will happen next.

Thinking About Ideas

1. Name two holidays that honor our past.
2. What special day is important to your family?
3. How do some people celebrate spring?
4. Name two symbols that stand for freedom.

Which special day do you like? Tell why.

Using Skills

Reviewing Using Calendars

1. Which month does this calendar show?

2. How many days are in this month?

3. What special day is celebrated on May 29?

4. When is Mother's Day?

Make Your Own!

- Write the name of a month on your calendar.
- Write the days of the week.
- Write the numbers for the days in the month.
- Add any holidays, birthdays, or other special days in the month.

Using Skills

Reviewing Making Predictions

Read to predict what happens next.

Today is Sally's birthday. Sally's
mother has a special present for her.
The present is hidden in a closet.
Sally's mother sees Sally about to
open the closet.

1. Make a prediction about what could
   happen if Sally opens the closet.
2. What do you think Sally's mother will say
   to Sally?
3. What do you think Sally will say to her
   mother?

UNIT PROJECT

Make a Card for a Special Day

- Choose a special day.
- Fold a sheet of paper in half.
- Draw a picture about a special day on the front of your card.
- Add pictures inside your card.
- Find the day on the calendar. Write the date.
- Send your card to someone special.

Reading on Your Own

You can look for these books at your library.

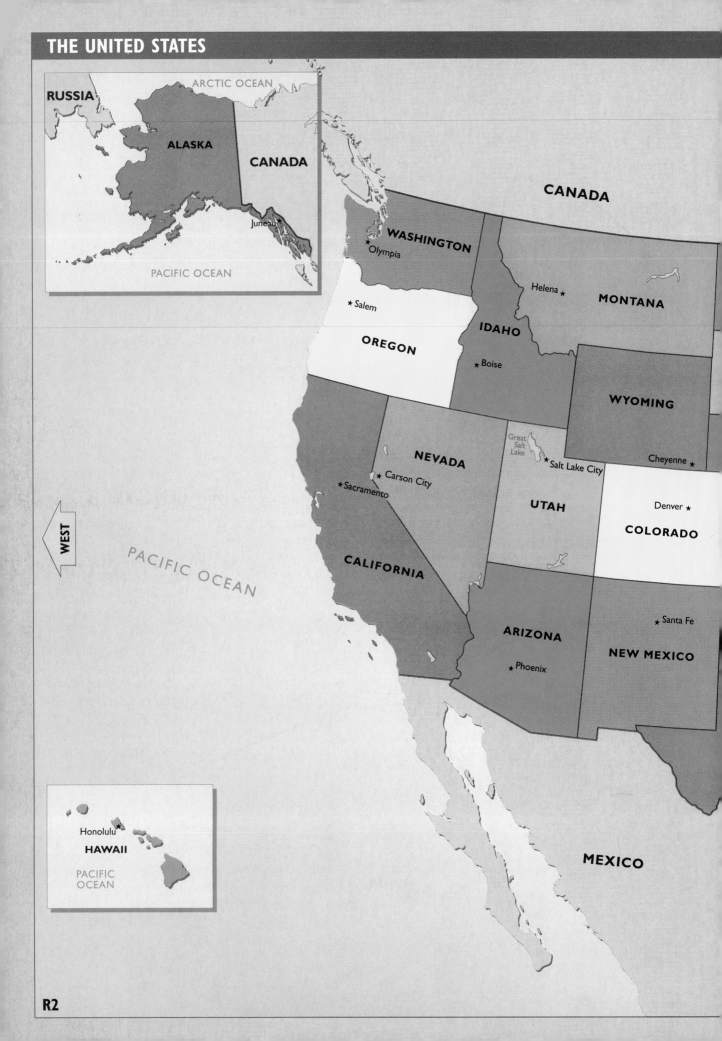

THE UNITED STATES

RUSSIA

ARCTIC OCEAN

ALASKA

CANADA

Juneau ★

PACIFIC OCEAN

CANADA

WASHINGTON

Olympia ★

Helena ★

MONTANA

★ Salem

IDAHO

OREGON

★ Boise

WYOMING

Cheyenne ★

NEVADA

Great Salt Lake

★ Salt Lake City

★ Carson City

★ Sacramento

UTAH

Denver ★

COLORADO

WEST

PACIFIC OCEAN

CALIFORNIA

ARIZONA

★ Santa Fe

NEW MEXICO

★ Phoenix

Honolulu

HAWAII

PACIFIC OCEAN

MEXICO

NORTH

CANADA

MAINE

NORTH DAKOTA
★ Bismarck

MINNESOTA

Lake Superior

MICHIGAN

Lake Huron

★ Augusta

Montpelier ★

VERMONT   NEW
          HAMPSHIRE
          ★ Concord

SOUTH DAKOTA
★ Pierre

WISCONSIN

St. Paul ★

Lake Michigan

Lansing ★

Lake Ontario

NEW
YORK

Albany ★

MASSACHUSETTS
           ★ Boston
           Providence

Hartford ★
CONNECTICUT   RHODE
              ISLAND

IOWA

Madison ★

Lake Erie

PENNSYLVANIA

Trenton ★
NEW JERSEY

NEBRASKA

Des Moines ★

ILLINOIS

Indianapolis ★

OHIO

Columbus ★

Harrisburg ★

Dover ★

Annapolis ★
            DELAWARE
            MARYLAND

Lincoln ★

Springfield ★

INDIANA

Frankfort ★

Washington,
D.C. ⊛

WEST
VIRGINIA ★ Charleston

VIRGINIA
Richmond ★

Topeka ★

MISSOURI

Jefferson
City ★

KENTUCKY

KANSAS

EAST

NORTH
CAROLINA   ★ Raleigh

★ Nashville

OKLAHOMA

ARKANSAS

TENNESSEE

★ Oklahoma
  City

Little
★ Rock

SOUTH
★ Columbia
CAROLINA

★ Atlanta

MISSISSIPPI

ALABAMA

GEORGIA

ATLANTIC OCEAN

TEXAS

LOUISIANA

★ Jackson

Montgomery ★

★ Tallahassee

★ Austin

Baton Rouge ★

FLORIDA

Gulf of Mexico

THE
BAHAMAS

⊛ National capital   ★ State capital

CUBA

SOUTH

R3

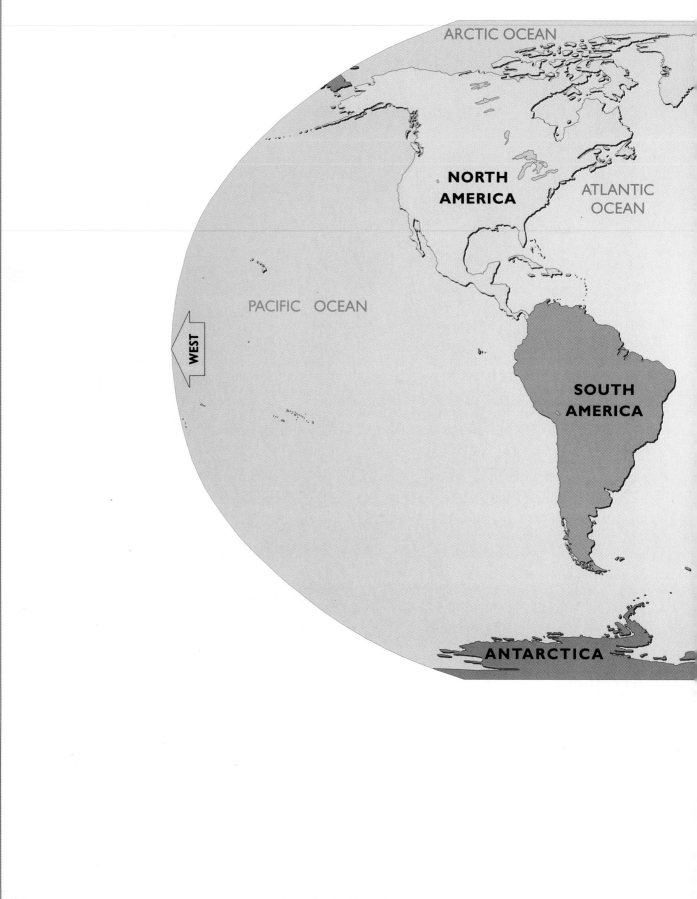

THE WORLD

NORTH

ARCTIC OCEAN

EUROPE

ASIA

PACIFIC OCEAN

AFRICA

EAST

INDIAN
OCEAN

ATLANTIC
OCEAN

AUSTRALIA

ANTARCTICA

SOUTH

Dictionary of GEOGRAPHIC WORDS

HILL Land that is higher than the land around it, but lower than a mountain.

PLAIN Flat land.

LAKE Body of water with land all around it.

ISLAND Land with water all around it.

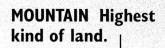

MOUNTAIN Highest kind of land.

RIVER Long body of water that flows across the land.

OCEAN Very big body of salt water.

PICTURE GLOSSARY

alike
These kittens look **alike**.
(page 50)

calendar
This **calendar** shows the month of May. (page 188)

celebrate
I will **celebrate** my seventh birthday. (page 190)

chart
The **chart** shows who won the game. (page 58)

citizen
Lara is a **citizen** of this country. So is Ken. (page 63)

community
Many neighborhoods make up a **community**. (page 16)

continent

North America is a **continent** on Earth. (page 118)

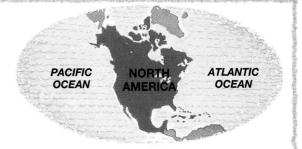

country

The United States of America is our **country**. (page 24)

different

My hat is **different** from Bill's. (page 50)

directions

North, south, east, and west are **directions** on a map. (page 108)

Earth

We call our world **Earth**. It has land and water. (page 27)

family

There are two children in Lola's **family**. (page 44)

goods
My dress, book, and this orange are **goods**. (page 76)

group
Fran and her friends are a **group**. (page 48)

hill
A **hill** is land that is higher than the land around it.
(page 105)

history
The story of America's past is called **history**. (page 147)

holiday
Flag Day is a **holiday** in June. (page 184)

job
My brother has a **job** in a store. (page 74)

lake

A **lake** is a body of water with land all around it.
(page 106)

law

It is a **law** to cross with the green light. (page 54)

main idea

The **main idea** tells what a story is about. (page 160)

map

You can find my school on this **map**. (page 9)

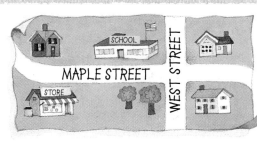

map key

A **map key** can help you read a map. (page 22)

mountain

A **mountain** is the highest kind of land. (page 105)

Native Americans

The first people to live in America are called Indians or **Native Americans**. (page 150)

natural resource

Water is a **natural resource** that people and animals use. (page 120)

needs

Food, clothing, shelter, and love are **needs**. (page 78)

neighborhood

People live, work, and play in my **neighborhood**. (page 7)

ocean

An **ocean** is a large body of salt water. (page 107)

order

Debby put the books in **order** from A to Z. (page 114)

picture graph
This **picture graph** shows how many red and blue crayons I have. (page 94)

Pilgrims
Pilgrims came to North America on the *Mayflower.*
(page 164)

plain
Our farm is on flat land called a **plain**. (page 104)

prediction
I made a **prediction** that it would rain. (page 194)

President
George Washington was our first **President**. (page 63)

river
A **river** is a long body of water that flows across the land. (page 106)

rule
It is a **rule** to raise your hand if you have a question.
(page 52)

season
Spring is a **season**.
(page 112)

service
My dad is a firefighter. He does a **service** for others.
(page 76)

settlement
The Pilgrims built a **settlement** at Plymouth.
(page 162)

settlers
Settlers built schools and farms. (page 162)

shelter
Our home is my family's **shelter**. (page 78)

sort
I like to **sort** things into groups. (page 88)

state

Texas is a **state** in our country. (page 24)

time line

Marcy's **time line** tells when she learned to swim. (page 148)

3 years old	5 years old	7 years old
Marcy learns to swim.	Marcy starts school.	Marcy joins soccer teams.

transportation

A school bus is a kind of **transportation**. (page 85)

volunteer

Jane's mom is a **volunteer** at the library. (page 77)

vote

Citizens can **vote** for a President. (page 60)

wants

This bike and skates are **wants**. (page 80)

weather

Sunshine brings warm **weather**. (page 110)

index

CREDITS

Cover: Pentagram

Maps: Geosystems

Illustrations: Ellen Appleby: pp 124-127, 202-203; Yvette Banek: pp 38, 68, 70, 98, 100, 138, 139(t), 140, 210, 212; Nan Brooks: pp 82-83; Randy Chewning: pp 84-87, 88, 89; Luisa D'Augusta: pp 96-97; Eldon Doty: pp 74, 75, 76, 77; Alyssa Gallo: pp 120-121; Michael Grejniec: pp 66-67; Meryl Henderson: pp 148, 149, 168, 169, 170, 171, 172, 179(t); Brian Karas: pp 48, 49, 56-57; Cheryl Kirk Knoll: pp 150-151; Alan Leiner: pp 165, 166, 167; Claude Martinot: pp 53; Karen Minot: pp R6-R7; Hima Pamoedjo: pp 21(m), 48-49, 69(t), 94, 95, 99(t), 191, 192, 193, 211(t); Rebecca Perry: pp 39(t), 40; Roz Schanzer: pp 30-37(border); Jerry Smath: pp R8-R15; Melissa Sweet: pp 176-177; Peggy Tagel: pp 23, 42-43, 72-73, 102-103, 142-143, 182-183; Mary Thelen: pp 208-209; Steve Sullivan: pp 54, 58, 59; Robert Van Nutt: pp 156-157, 158-159, 160, 161; Nina Wallace: pp 8, 9, 20-21, 22, 23

Thank you to all the children who contributed their work, including Alyssa Gallo, Brentin Gultz, Molly Mc Fadden, Paul Mitchell, Christopher Mitchell, Rita Munifo, and Mrs. Struzik's first grade class in Netcong, New Jersey.

PHOTOGRAPHY CREDITS: All photographs are by the Macmillan/McGraw-Hill School Division (MMSD) except as noted below.

Cover and i: Bob Esparza for MMSD. iii t.l. Grant Heilman/Grant Heilman Photography, Inc.; b.l. Jim Levin for MMSD. iv: t. Key Photos; m. Francis Westfield for MMSD; b. Runk Schoenberger/Grant Heilman Photography, Inc. v: t. Francis Westfield for MMSD; m. Bob Daemmrich/Stock Boston, Inc.; b. Uniphoto, Inc. vi: b. Francis Westfield for MMSD. x: t. Ric Ergenbright; b. Tom McCarthy/National Stock Network. xi: t. Elizabeth Wolf. xi: t.r. Joseph H. Bailey; m. Breton Littlehales; b.r. Joseph H. Bailey. **Unit 1** 2: Bob Jones, Jr/Liaison International. 3: l. Joe Viesti/Viesti Associates, Inc.; t.r. Tony Stone Images. 6–7: Mark A. Guerra for MMSD. 10: l. David Meunch; r. John Feingersh/The Stock Market. 11: Lionel Delevingne/Stock Boston, Inc. 12: Mark A. Guerra for MMSD. 13: James Levin. 14-15: Andy Sacks for MMSD. 15: l. Andy Sacks for MMSD; r. Phil Degginger/Bruce Coleman. 16: Loren Irving. 17: Superstock. 18: Bob Jones, Jr/Liaison International. 19: b. John Henley/Uniphoto; t. John Feingersh. 20: Albert J. Gordon/Profiles West. 22: t.l. Grant Heilman/Grant Heilman Photography, Inc.; b.l. C.J. Allen/Stock Boston. 25: Richard Hirneisen for MMSD. 26: r., b.r. R. Larry Lefever/Grant Heilman Photography, Inc. 28: t.l. Margarette Mead/The Image Bank; t.m. Ken Karp for MMSD; b. Runk Schoenberger/Grant Heilman Photography, Inc. v: t. Bruce Caines for MMSD; t.r. E.R. Degginger/Bruce Coleman, Inc.; m.r , b.m. Scott Harvey for MMSD; b.r. Titus Kana for MMSD; r. L.D. Gordon/The Image Bank; l. Mulvehill/The Image Works. 29: t.r. Ken Karp for MMSD; t. Ed Bock/The Stock Market; b.r. Karen Ann Wilson/Natural Selection; b.m. Gamma Liaison; m.l. Bill Waltzen for MMSD; b.l. Ken Karp for MMSD. 41: Monica Stevenson for MMSD. **Unit 2** 42: t.l. Terry Farmer/Tony Stone Images; b.l. Lori Adamski Peek/Tony Stone Images. 44–45: Francis Westfield for MMSD. 46–47: l. Superstock. 47: l. Elliott Smith. 48: b.l. Don Klumpp; b.r. Paul Miller/Black Star; t. Jim Levin for MMSD. 49: t.r. Wayne Eastep/Tony Stone Images; t.l. Lawrence Migdale; b. Jim Levin for MMSD. 50: t. Lawrence Migdale; b. Superstock. 51: b. Peter Correz/Tony Stone Worldwide; t. Tomas del Ano/Adstock Photos. 52: Jim Levin for MMSD. 53: Francis Westfield for MMSD. 54: Jim Levin for MMSD. 55: t.r. Sam Sargent/Liaison International; m.r. C. Podias/ FPG International; b.r. Patrick Eden/The Image Bank; m. Jim Levin for MMSD. 60–62: Jim Levin for MMSD. 63: Cynthia Johnson/Gamma-Liaison. 64: l. Key Photos; b.r. Michael S. Yamashita/The Stock House, Ltd. 65: t. Karen Kasmauski/Woodfin Camp & Associates. 71: Monica Stevenson for MMSD. **Unit 3** 72: t.l. Jeff Dunn/The Picture Cube; t.r. Bob Abraham/The Stock Market; m.r. Michael Heron/Woodfin Camp; b.m. Richard Kolar/Animals Animals. 73: b.l. Eric Roth/The Picture Cube; t. Juan Pablo Lira/The Image Bank. 74–75: Francis Westfield. 76: b. David Young Wolff/Photo Edit; t. Thomas Del Brase/The Stock Market. 77: l. Charles Gupton/Tony Stone International; r. Francis Westfield for MMSD. 78: l. Francis Westfield for MMSD; r. Ulf Sjostedt/FPG International. 79–81: Francis Westfield for MMSD. 84: Courtesy of The Oshkosh Public Museum. 85: l. Beringer-Dratch/The Picture Cube; r. John Terence Turner/FPG. 86: t. Tony Stone Worldwide; b. Alan Pitcairn/Grant Heilman. 87: t. Peter Cole/Bruce Coleman; b. Peter Gridley/FPG International. 88, 90: Francis Westfield for MMSD. 91: t. Kay Chernush/The Image Bank; b. Cameramann International. 92–94: Francis Westfield for MMSD. 101: Monica Stevenson for MMSD. **Unit 4** 104: b. , t.r. Francis Westfield for MMSD; m. Tom Bean/The Stock Market. 105: t. Hans Wendler/The Image Bank; b. Ken Graham/Tony Stone Images. 106: t.l. Berenholtz/The Stock Market; m.r. David Weintraub/Photo Researchers; b.l. James P. Blair/National Geographic Society Image Collection; t.r. Francis Westfield for MMSD. 107: t.r. Francis Westfield/Photo Researchers; b. Runk Schoenberger/Grant Heilman. 108: b. Francis Westfield for MMSD; t. Runk Schoenberger/Grant Heilman. 110: t.r. Francis Westfield for MMSD; b.r. Bill Frantz/Tony Stone Images. 110-111: bkgnd. Francis Westfield for MMSD. 111: Francis Westfield for MMSD. 112: l. Jan Halaska/Photo Researchers; r. Jan Halaska/Photo Researchers. 112-113: Francis Westfield for MMSD. 113: Jan Halaska/Photo Researchers. 114–115: Francis Westfield for MMSD. 117: t.l. Francis Westfield for MMSD; b.r. Will & Deni McIntyre/Tony Stone Images; t.r. M. Macri/Masterfile. 120-121: bkgnd. Francis Westfield for MMSD. 120: l. David R. Frazier Photo Library. 121: r. Renee Lynn/Photo Researchers. 122: m.l., b.l. Francis Westfield for MMSD; t.m. Gary Buss/FPG International; b.m. Don Smetzer/Tony Stone Images. 122-123: Francis Westfield for MMSD. 123: t.l. John Mead/SPL/Photo Researchers; t.r. Dennis Brack/Black Star; b.r. Susan Pfannmuller/Midwestock. 124: l. Francis Westfield for MMSD; r. Cathlyn Melloan/Tony Stone Images. 125: r. Vanessa Vick/Photo Researchers, Inc. 126: Francis Westfield for MMSD. 127: t.l. Michael Krasowitz/FPG International; r. Francis Westfield for MMSD. 128-129: Grant Heilman Photography. 128: m. Monica Stevenson for MMSD; b.r., t.r. Ralph W. Sanders for MMSD; t.m. Monica Stevenson for MMSD. 129: t.l., t.r. Ralph W. Sanders for MMSD; b.r. Monica Stevenson for MMSD. 141: Monica Stevenson for MMSD. **Unit 5** 142: t. The Granger Collection; m.r. Mark E. Gibson; t. The Granger Collection. 143: m. Uniphoto, Inc. 145: t.l. courtesy C. A. Powell. 147: t. Nicholas Conte/Bruce Coleman, Inc.; b.l. H. Armstrong Roberts; r. Bob Daemmrich/Stock Boston. 152: Michael McDermott for MMSD. 153: t. Colorado Historical Society. 155: l. Phil Schofield/AllStock; b.r. Monty Roessel. 156: t.l. The Granger Collection. 162: Mark E. Gibson. 163: Myron Wood/Photo Researchers. 164: John Ulven/Plimoth Plantation. 166: Candace Cochrane/Positive Images. 168: l. Baltimore Historical Society. 169–170: The Granger Collection. 171: The Bettmann Archive. 172: t. Archive/Levick; l. Rafael Macia/Photo Researchers, Inc. 173: m. Francis Westfield for MMSD. 178: b.l. The Granger Collection; l. Uniphoto Picture Agency. 181: Monica Stevenson for MMSD. **Unit 6** 182: b.r. The Bettmann Archives; r. Bettmann Newsphotos. 184: The Granger Collection. 185: t. Stephen Agricola/Folio; r. Wes Thompson/The Stock Market. 186: The Bettmann Archives. 187: t. Andre Jenny/Unicorn Stock Photos; b. Peter Gridley/FPG International. 190-191: Stan Ries. 191: t. John M. Roberts/The Stock Market. 192: t. Fotografia Prod./J. Houck/Westlight; t. Stuart L. Craig, Jr/Bruce Coleman. 193: b.r. Aneal Vohra/Unicorn Stock photos; b.l. Flip Schulke. 194: Monica Stevenson for MMSD. 195: Superstock. 196: l. Monica Stevenson for MMSD; l. Superstock; r. Monica Stevenson for MMSD; r. Jeffrey W. Myers/Stock Boston. 197: l., t. Monica Stevenson for MMSD; b. Susan Lampton for MMSD; t. Mug Shots/The Stock Market. 198-199: Monica Stevenson for MMSD. 200-201: Monica Stevenson for MMSD. 200: l., r. courtesy of Project Bridge/Houston. 201: r. Monica Stevenson for MMSD; l. courtesy of Project Bridge/ Houston. 202: l. Gamma-Liaison; r. Superstock. 203: l. James P. Blair/National Geographic Society; r. Odyssey/Frerck/Chicago. 204: Uniphoto, Inc. 204-205: Monica Stevenson for MMSD. 205: t. Norman Owen Tomalin/Bruce Coleman; b. Monica Stevenson for MMSD. 206: b. Jeff Vanuga/Westlight; t. Monica Stevenson for MMSD. 206-207: Monica Stevenson for MMSD. 207: Anne Nielsen for MMSD. 213: Monica Stevenson for MMSD. Endpapers: Bridgeman Art Library.

(continued from page ii)

Acknowledgments

"The World is Big, The World is Small" by Ella Jenkins. Copyright 1966 by River Bend Music, Inc. (ASCAP) assigned 1968 to Ella Jenkins, Chicago, Il.
"Money's Funny" from **Nuts to You and Nuts to Me** by Mary Ann Hoberman. Copyright 1974 by Mary Ann Hoberman. Gina Maccoby Literary Agency.
"What Was It Like" from **Snippets** by Charlotte Zolotow. Copyright 1993 by Charlotte Zolotow. HarperCollins Publishers.